Blessed With Cancer

JACK RHODES

Footprint Publications

ISBN-10: 1727343638
ISBN-13: 978-1727343632

DEDICATION

Dedicated to Patti and my loving family, and to all the people who work daily with cancer patients and towards it's cure.

Jack Rhodes

CONTENT

Jack Rhodes

ACKNOWLEDGMENTS

I would be remorse if I did not thank the people who made this book possible.

1. My Lord and Savior Jesus Christ, who through Him all things are possible.

2. My loving wife Patti, the most unselfish person I have ever met. My loving children, Nate, Sarah, David, and Tim. My very supportive siblings, Mike and Cheryl, who encouraged me through some very dark times. My extended family who always called with words of support, especially Jessica, who had a knack for a much needed uplift.

3. To all of my friends mentioned in my book, who always made my life a better place. God blessed me through all of you.

4. The countless people who encouraged me to complete this book. In particular, Lynn Salyer and David Lee, who with their unselfish assistance made the book possible.

5. Finally, the surgeons and nurses of the Cleveland Clinic, who made it possible for me to be in the five percentile of advanced colon cancer survivors.

Jack Rhodes

FORWARD

Four years ago, Jack Rhodes walked into my office for an evaluation of a large incisional hernia, which developed after the first couple of the many operations he has undergone over the past few years. Immediately the two of us hit it off. Jack was funny, kind, and had such a positive attitude after all that he had been through. Surprisingly, I remember that he was also uncomfortable taking his shirt off to show me his hernia. I did not realize it then, but to this patient, the scars across his abdomen served as a constant reminder of the cancer and the way it had already affected his life. Jack was just at the beginning of his journey to accept his diagnosis, and ultimately consider it a blessing. It also was the beginning of our friendship.

Mr. Rhodes was diagnosed with appendicitis, a very common and treatable disease. However, everything changed when ultimately it was determined that he actually had colon cancer and he would have to deal with the very significant ramifications. In this book, Jack so eloquently describes all that cancer has taken away but it also eventually reveals all that the experience has given to him. As surgeons, we tend to see things in black and white, when in reality our world is many shades of gray. We may see patients every few weeks or every few months, but this book describes the day-to-day struggles and the small victories that all patients face, along with their friends and family.

Jack's story truly begins in the operating room where he is brought face-to-face with the realization that his life was no longer under his control. His survival suddenly was now in the hands of a complete stranger, a surgeon that he could only hope did not fall asleep during colon removal class in medical school! Indeed this single moment reveals the awesome power and responsibility that we have as physicians, yet it also reveals the humbling vulnerability that all of our patients face.

A planned five day hospitalization becomes a two-month ordeal. Eventually recovering, Jack takes the reader through the celebration of the short-lived remission and then the devastating news that the cancer had recurred. Ultimately, Mr. Rhodes comes to the sobering realization that he will never again be cancer free.

With the acceptance of his diagnosis, Jack now understands that he has no control over whether or not he was going to die. However, he could have complete control over how he would live. He suddenly is able to take back his independence by being more involved in his care. He studies the different treatment regimens and helps with decisions, he eats right, and he drinks lots of water. Jack again starts to appreciate the glorious little things in life, such as watching squirrels in his backyard and the beautiful views of Lake Erie.

With the support of his friends and his family, Mr. Rhodes takes back his life. He spends time with those that he loves. He commiserates with friends. He gives advice to others. He has learned to live with the blessing of cancer. In an act of defiance to his disease, Mr. Rhodes now easily takes off his shirt and realizes that the scars are an integral part of who he ultimately is. His badge of courage. His declaration that cancer would not define him.

Early on, Jack's wise neighbor told him that he had to have a purpose, a reason to get up in the morning. This book is exactly that... the description of the long road to acceptance of his diagnosis, the thank you note to his friends and colleagues who touched his life, the declaration of his Christian beliefs, the comfort of knowing that his mother, who passed away long ago, was watching over him, and most importantly, this is a love letter to his family and especially to his wife Patti.

We, as readers, are all so fortunate to be a part of Jack's journey.

Dr. Steven Rosenblatt M.D.

Cleveland Clinic

INTRODUCTION

*I*know you are scared, I was too and quite frankly I still am. I wasn't surprised nor did I feel like I was kicked in the stomach when I heard the words you have cancer, but I also didn't know how long the road ahead was going to be either. There were no road maps for me to follow. The best advice I received was from a random physician at the Cleveland Clinic who told me I was now in a marathon, not a sprint. My family bought books to help guide me through the process, but everything I was reading was either from a doctor's point of view or a guide to get my spiritual life in order. Nothing prepared me for what my immediate future had in store. You are going through a major life crisis and there is no preparation. The best intended physicians still are oblivious to the fact that most patients have no understanding what they are saying or the instructions they are giving. Since my diagnosis I have had more than my share of friends who have been diagnosed. They all call me with the same questions as they too are unfamiliar with what they should be doing and what is in store for their future. All cancer is different and even the same cancer is different in each patient but there are a few things to minimize the side effects and keep yourself strong through the process.

This is my story with my thoughts and my experiences. The story is unique, even for a cancer patient. I battled cancer on several fronts as I had seven surgeries in less than three years. My initial chemotherapy treatment began with twenty two sessions. I then tried various other treatments including chemotherapy and non-conventional options throughout my fight with cancer. I was fighting the fight with no guidance from other people who traveled the route. This book is designed to help other patients diagnosed with cancer. This has to be a straight talk dialogue as many of us share a common bond of the unknown. I learned in my youth an old proverb which states "learn from the mistakes of others, you will not live long enough to make them all yourself". The common denominator among all cancer patients is that unknown and wanting to know what to expect with the fight ahead.

When I was diagnosed I knew that I was in for the fight for my life. I heard the stories of chemotherapy but didn't know the extent of its long term effects and the challenges associated with it. What I didn't expect were the many blessings I received from the result of the disease. I lived in a day-to-day lifestyle like most of us do. We had dinner with friends and family and had our share of holiday fatigue with family. I had no idea that cancer would open my eyes and heart in a way which would prove to be so profound and life changing. Cancer is a struggle and is not fun by any stretch of the imagination. I became so blessed by being aware of my friends and family's behavior. Their unabashed love for me which I must have taken for granted prior to the diagnosis. There are many books on staying positive which, as a sales manager, I have read every one. The depth of its meaning never struck home until I faced this fight of my life. I no longer sweat the small stuff and appreciate the little things around me. I began to feed the squirrels and birds in the backyard and appreciated their beauty as God's creatures. I truly became blessed because of cancer.

Just because I became aware of nature's beauty did not mean I could relax in my fight against a relentless foe. You will be in a fight! Ask questions and be proactive. Most oncologist are reacting to what they find but may put off surgery or more testing until the condition manifests itself further. Remember, the earlier you treat the cancer the better chance of a full recovery. This includes any metastasis. My brother who is a kidney cancer survivor told me his doctor wanted to wait to see if the cancer grew before addressing the issues. He did not accept that approach and luckily changed physicians who suggested immediate surgery. He is now cancer free and living a normal life. There are a lot of great physicians but you need to be proactive in your own therapy. There are so many learning curves in your battle but this is one you will need to establish almost immediately.

It is so important to stay positive and just know cancer CAN be curable. A nurse can tell who is going to live the longest just by their outward personality and determination to fight the battle. If a patient is upbeat and positive they swear it lengthens the life span. It is easy to stay in bed and you would be justified in living the "poor me" lifestyle. No one would blame you. It was at this time I developed my motto in my personal fight. I told my family, "cancer may take my life but it was not going to take a day away from me". I was going to live my life daily. Sometimes it was a battle to just get out of bed, let alone out of the house, but that was my daily goal. I believe this daily goal has extended my life significantly.

Be prepared for those negative people around you who mean well. Try to change their thought pattern or eliminate them from your inner circle. Keep your family informed as they are the best support system you have. If there are no family members, try to get your friends or church involved to help. Sometimes you just need a sounding board, but other times you will need help with daily activities. As soon as you are diagnosed, begin establishing your support system. It is equally important for your inner strength as well as your outward needs.

"Blessed with Cancer" appears to be an oxymoron of how you should feel when first diagnosed with cancer. I was going through life, like most people, one day at a time always looking ahead or looking to the past. Once I was diagnosed, I discovered my true friends and family members who really cared about me. The people who knew my surgery dates, appointments and would call to see how I was doing. It made me appreciate life daily. I began to enjoy the little things around me which we normally do not see. The wonderment of life is all around us and should be enjoyed whether you are blessed with cancer or not.

1

IT WAS JUST A TYPICAL DAY

I am much like your typical person. I would hear a story about a person with back pain who died a month later with advanced cancer and knew that is what I had. Our friends would compare our aches and pains like a scene from "Everyone Loves Raymond". However, we were all healthy and having fun in our early retirement years. We are very active to the point our adult children can no longer keep up and have no problem driving an hour for lunch. In fact, I think they are glad to see us leave after a weekend visit as they need some time to rest.

I have to backtrack a little to the point when I married Patti, the most beautiful person I have ever met after my recent divorce. In my eyes, she was not only beautiful on the outside but the most selfless, fun loving person I have ever met. I finally got this part of my life right. She loved my four kids and they loved and accepted her. Her youngest just went off to college but she was not ready to be an empty nester. I know this is a rare prospect of a life change but there was instant bonding which made our transition very easy. At the time we met my children were covering every gamut of life. Nathan was in his final year of college and was pretty much on his own. He was in his final year of Air Force ROTC with his career path already mapped. He went to the University of Toledo for business but after one year knew he wanted to pursue his dream of becoming a pilot. We had a serious Father to Son planning session as he came to me for advice. He is my oldest and behaved like you would expect from the oldest. He is an overachiever who never procrastinated. He was the type of son who would take the trash out when he saw it was full rather than wait to be told. He wanted to be a pilot and an alternate plan was needed. We both offered suggestions and looked at the solutions like we were in any business board room. He quickly decided on the quickest plan of action, ROTC. He graduated and instantly went into the Air Force where he became a pilot on the KC-135. Upon retirement he was hired by Southwest Airlines as a pilot and started on February 9th, my birthday. Sarah, my only daughter, was just starting her senior year of high school and was in much need of a mother. Her real mother was battling mental illness and was sometimes present physically but not there in spirit. Patti was more than happy to fill the role. They got along well, as Sarah is much like Patti, always wanting to do the right thing. Patti was there for her throughout her years of college, marriage and the birth of her two children. Sarah is the easiest person to be around and she and Patti quickly developed a strong bond. Sarah was delighted as she could wear Patti's outfits, which now doubled her wardrobe. Patti was more than happy to share as she was getting the daughter she always wanted and Sarah was definitely the perfect daughter for her. David was entering his sophomore year with a promising career in sports. He was on the bubble to be a starter on an undefeated football team from the year before. Although he was a superior athlete, his high school football career was cut short with a broken leg both his junior and senior years. He was still athletic enough to earn a full football scholarship to McKendree College, a smaller college in Illinois. After graduation he went to work in the Boston area. He worked on his Masters and continued his education at UMass and Harvard. He quickly became manager of the east coast for his company at age thirty four. Tim was an eighth grader and more than happy to have someone do his laundry and pick up after him as he was the youngest and need I say more. He is the child with the most promise though! We called Tim the Senator because of his outgoing personality and loud booming voice. He graduated from Bowling Green State University but wanted to stay close to home and became a salesman for a Ford dealership. Patti had two boys, TJ and Kyle, which fit in well with my family as they were in the same social circles as my two oldest. They knew each other and I knew who they were before I met their mother. They are a little more introverted than I am and they took a while to get used to my hugs. Big hugs is my family's way to say hello or goodbye, but it was a bit awkward at first. It was kind of funny as they knew I liked to hug and I knew they didn't. They would adjust to giving me a hug while I was adjusting to them by sticking my hand out to shake theirs.

Our family was like most families, full of chaos of jam-packed schedules running the kids to maintain their commitments. Each of the kids were so active both athletically and scholastically. When I was in school I always found more time for social activities than my grades and didn't want my kids to have some of the same regrets I have had in my life. I always stressed the basic pyramid of education. I was always preaching, you have to understand and conquer each block of the pyramid to get to the top. Each grade was important, each class was important as it was the basis for your next grade or your next class. It was the same in athletics. Conquer the basics before you try the next step. Once the basics become second nature the next step is easy. Build upon each block and go on to the next block until you reach the sky. I stressed to first become the best on your team. Then become the best in your city, and then the best in our part of the state, but above all, use the sport don't let the sport use you. This simple foundation has served me well through my professional life as well. As a father, I have made some mistakes raising my children but thank goodness there were no permanent scars. I always believed the best thing you can do for your children is to pass on your strong beliefs. Your time to teach so swiftly passes so you have to make every moment count.

My mother passed away from ovarian cancer when I was six, just a week before my first grade. Consequently, I grew up with an acute understanding of the finite time we have together. I wanted to make my time with my children special by being available. We would try to have a family outing every weekend, even if it was just to go to the mall. We were like the Brady Bunch as the kids all got along and enjoyed those little excursions. We didn't have much money so most trips were to the park or other free adventures. Dinner on the town was usually a trip to the buffet table where they charged by how old the kids were. That was all we could afford, but it was fun. We stressed family values and when they were on their own, hoped all of our teachings would paid off.

My second youngest son, David, had a tough decision to make his senior year. He was a much sought after defensive back in football. He was being followed by the top colleges in the country even after breaking a leg his junior year. His senior year was filled with anticipation as the colleges were calling every night, but then he broke his opposite leg in the third game. The recruiters backed off except for a small NAIA school who offered him a full scholarship. He always wanted to play in the big arena and knew he was capable but the larger programs were only offering a preferred walk-on status with no scholarship guarantees. My life long guidance was "use the sport, don't let the sport use you". There is such a small percentage of athletes to go professional, the odds were against him. Rob Lytle was a very close friend of mine who was an All-American at Michigan and later played for the Denver Broncos. I saw the toll the sport took on his body and secretly hoped my kids would never made it that far. Rob was the epitome of a football player. He worked hard and did what the coaches asked from him. At less than 200 pounds he played fullback at Michigan when Bo Schembechler asked him to switch from tailback. When he turned fifty-six he told me the average age of death of a retired football player was fifty six. He passed away of a heart attack within two weeks of our conversation. He was very adamant regarding the concussion investigation and its long term effect on the body, in particular, the brain. He also felt the concussions were related to the many retired athletes who suffered heart attacks and strokes. I reflected on our conversation at his funeral and although he appreciated the crowds, I wondered if he would have done it the same way if given the chance. After all my direction through the years, Dave decided to take the bird in the hand and go to the smaller school. It was a tough decision for him but he didn't let the sport use him. He used the sport and graduated with no loans and a wonderful education.

The empty nest was upon us and we didn't know what hit us. No more practices, plays, concerts and games. We were able to schedule a little time for ourselves. It was nice but we are very active people and found we were scheduling lunches 50 miles away because we heard it was good from the food channel. It was a great life with the exception the kids ended up on opposite ends of the country. Their professional life took them too far away from me. I had one in Boston, one in Phoenix the other two stayed in our home town of Fremont, Ohio. Patti's children settled in Austin, TX and Columbus, Ohio, all great places to visit! Although we were both still working, our lives were settling in to a routine of travel, fun, family and friends. We are social people and always on the move. We are not big party animals but don't stay home often either. We just loved being together regardless of the event. We enjoyed taking a drive as much as going out for a night on the town. Of course our night on the town was now home by eleven.

This is how our lives maintained until that day in November 2013. A few weeks earlier we were vacationing in Florida and I had a sharp pain over my appendix. I instantly went to the Internet to look up appendicitis. I found the symptom for appendicitis is increasing pain. My pain decreased so thought it must be a hernia. The next morning the pain was gone but decided to set an appointment with my family doctor as well as my urologist. I was always on a maintenance schedule to the point where I felt I would never die since I was taking such great care of my body! I always had this intense fear of dying since I was nine years old. I can remember it vividly as the thought of forever and eternity scared the heck out of this little kid. I was raised in a semi-strict Catholic home, attending St Joseph Catholic grade school. The priest and sisters of Notre Dame could preach fire and brimstone better than any TV evangelist. My religion classes consisted of sessions on the descriptions of eternity. It seemed like a very long time to a nine year old who felt last Christmas was ancient history. Ever since my mom passed away of ovarian cancer when I was six, death became very real and permanent to me. Death just didn't seem so very far away as my grandparents, and other aunts and uncles died within several years of my mom. It made me realize at a very young age, never go to bed angry and always kiss your family goodbye. We were so serious about the kissing part, that I would kiss my dad goodbye if I was going to the neighborhood store for a loaf of bread. Consequently, we became a very close family and still are to this day. My dad was a widower at age 39 but never remarried. He said he married the love of his life and knew no one could replace her. I never really knew the difference as a kid as your reality is the present. I never really thought about not having a mom as my dad filled the role. He really never opened up regarding the loss of my mom until his later years. He would talk about her pain and how agonizing it was for him to helplessly watch her digress. Cancer is still a mystery but in 1960 the treatment was almost barbaric. There was little known about the illness and even less about the cure and treatment. I can remember at one time her treatment was a heat lamp on her back. We have made great strides but at that time cancer was mostly a death sentence.

I was fairly certain my family physician would examine me, say take two aspirins and call me in the morning type of response. I was afraid he would begin to think of me as a hypochondriac after he would send me away. I almost didn't go to the appointment but Patti insisted we go. Once in his office he gave me a cursory glance and said he didn't see anything and told me to watch the area and come back if anything persist. As I walked out I began to regret setting the appointment as I am sure I was right, he thought I was a hypochondriac. It almost made me wish he found something so I would not look like such a baby. My appointment with my Urologist was the very next day and they did the normal prostate examine and suggested a CTSCAN in case my pain derived from a shifting kidney stone. I declined as I didn't want both physicians to think I was a hypochondriac. They were kind and suggested any time I am in the area to come back and I would be at the head of the line for the scan if I so desired. The following week we were within a block of the urologist office so Patti suggested I just go ahead and get the scan as I had nothing to lose. It took less than ten minutes and we were on to our plans for the day. We met our daughter to look at a possible new house and off to the local pizza pub for dinner. I didn't have a care in the world as I was feeling fine and knew it was just an inexplicable pain. Nothing to worry about. We were fast asleep when I woke to the phone ringing, which historically has never been a positive phone call. It was the radiologist who asked if I was in the emergency room at the hospital. I was somewhat amused and said no. He said the scan indicated I had a ruptured appendix and should immediately go to the emergency room if I begin to feel any pain, otherwise check into the hospital in the morning. We compromised and went to the emergency room the next morning. We had just bought a new mattress and I wanted to sleep on it so I thought everything else could wait. I did have a great night sleep and was looking forward to seeing if the bed would be as nice that night as well. Little did I know it would be two months before I would get a second night sleep on that mattress!

2

THE WIRLWIND OF DISCOVERY

We checked into the emergency room at the Toledo hospital for a ruptured appendix and was immediately put into the surgery rotation. The emergency room was full of activity which most emergency rooms are. I was fitted in my gown, completed all the paperwork and accessed with an IV. We waited and thought they forgot about us several times. They had a large number of people coming and going but would check periodically, informing me there was another emergency which put my surgery back. It was now becoming late afternoon on a Friday and I knew the emergency room would get very active on a weekend night. This went on until 6:00 pm when the surgeon came in to inform me I was next. She was surprised I was in no pain as she was expecting a delirious patient. She said she wanted the radiologist to review my scan as I should be in severe pain. This was not normal for a person waiting for a ruptured appendix surgery. She checked me further and decided to admit me for the night and would evaluate me again the next morning. Something wasn't right but I had no idea what the situation could be.

We had to call Sarah, our daughter, as she was the one we called when going into the hospital that morning. She lived in our hometown and was the one person we always checked with to let her know where we were. Patti and I are social people who would take a weekend trip on a whim. Sarah would get so concerned we had to promise to check with her when making our plans.

We thought the hospital scenario was comical as we were sure they made a mistake and I would be released early the next morning. This was not the case and our comical scenario was just the beginning of the whirlwind which was about to engulf us. The doctor entered the hospital room with a very sober face and bluntly said it was not a ruptured appendix but a cancerous tumor on my colon. They would have to retest, but surgery would be needed. Chemotherapy was discussed but was in the future. It all happened fast but I was not in a state of shock or even taken aback. I have always been my most calm when things were at its worst. I remember when David was ten he was dunking a basketball at a friend's house on those adjustable hoops. He was laughing when he was dunking and caught his front teeth on the net and ripped his pallet in two places. The ambulance driver told me he has worked many accidents including motorcycle injuries and never saw anything like this. I was panicking inside and the x-ray technician offered little hope as she told me she has never seen anything like this in her twenty years performing x-rays. This was just the reassurance a parent wants to hear when their ten year old is laying in a pool of blood. I remained calm and collected and drove him forty five miles talking to him the whole way in a very calm voice. Once he was in surgery I cried like a baby.

I knew my situation was very serious and began to realize the situation was life threatening. Patti insisted the Cleveland Clinic was the place to go for colon surgery. I asked for the opportunity of a second opinion and the doctor was very gracious and even called the clinic herself on my behalf. Patti took over and was able to work her way to the right people. They said they would admit me that night. They suggested I be transported by ambulance but we had our car and we promised to drive ourselves immediately to the clinic in Cleveland. We promised we would drive directly to the main building of the Cleveland Clinic. Of course we went straight to the house for pajamas and toiletries as we were sure I would be staying four or five days. Our son, Tim, was at the house and kept trying to reassure Patti everything would be fine. It was a comical sight as she was running around trying to gather things she thought she would need for the hospital stay, but he was trying to hug her to calm her down. This made her more restless as time was important. We promised to drive directly to the hospital and the staff was waiting for our arrival. Each of us were handling the crisis, which had just hit the family, in their own unique fashion.

The hour drive to the clinic gave us ample time to reflect on the seriousness of the news and what may lie ahead. We checked in and they were able to put us in a private room but not on the colorectal floor. They would begin testing within the next few days. They wanted to perform their own set of test. They told me it was not that they did not trust the results of the other hospital but they wanted to perform additional tests as well as verify the original results.

It was two days of colonoscopy, x-rays, blood draws and scans. It was confirmed it was a tumor on the bottom of my ascending colon. The worst possible site for survival. The only way I knew this was a doctor was discussing my situation and told me the closer to the anus the best chance of early recovery. Once he finished with his explanation, he asked where my tumor was located. Yes, it was the furthest point away from the anus it could get. His face went blank, but we both just chuckled. This was the hard-luck story of my family as far as I can remember. I don't want to sound negative, but it was true. If something could go wrong, it happened to the Rhodes family. I heard a story about one of my ancestors who came from Scotland made the trip to New York but was mugged and lost all his possessions. They then worked hard for two years to secure enough money to raft their way to their remaining family in Chicago. They made it as far as Ohio where their raft fell apart in Lake Erie. Wisely they decided to settle in Ohio where the family remains to this day. We do learn our lessons. It just seems like strange things happen to our family but we develop through the adversity with determination and strong work ethic. This time it is going to be up to the surgeons.

Nothing could prepare me for all the thoughts and insecurities of knowing your actual life is out of your control. It is now in the hands of a complete stranger who you hope didn't fall asleep in colon removal classes. The Cleveland Clinic and particularly my surgeon, Hermann Kessler, were very sensitive to our fears and reservations of the surgery. He was painstakingly direct and deliberate in his explanation of the surgery and possible outcomes. My family was at my side and always participated in the physician meetings to discuss options, outcomes and the changes in our future. It was a very sober time for me as there were many things which could go wrong. We have never faced this type of decision-making in our family. It was new ground for all of us and I was proud there was no pessimism from anyone, only pure optimism. I was gaining strength from my family, a role reversal for me. I also tried to be the heart of the family but looking into the faces of my adult children I realized the role is being reversed. It was me who was gaining the optimism from them. They were giving me the strength and hope going into this surgery. They were all by my side, but my constant companion was Patti. I never knew her to have such strength and resolve. She was not leaving my side. Patti was incredible as she had the dubious task of coordinating and balancing all the kids' visits, personalities, questions and feedback. Sarah stepped in to help coordinate the bookkeeping and be the information specialist. She would be the contact person with our friends who were trying to offer encouragement while getting updates. Sarah has her Masters in nursing and understood what the doctors were explaining to us. They would explain in doctor language and she in turn spoke English to us. Sarah also made the cutest sign which she hung on my hospital room door. It read "Enter here to meet the world's best dad & Papack. Please handle with care." The grandchildren call me Papack. I love it as no one else was called Papack. It originated from my grandson, Carter, who couldn't say Grandpa Jack, which is what the older grandchildren called me at the time. It came out Papack which has stuck ever since. Although our grandchildren are spread out across the country we remained very close. My children stress the importance of our paternal order of the family to their children. Not to mention I am a perpetual twelve year old and they love it when we visit them. They know it is going to be a week of getting away with everything and never ending travels of fun.

I had to have a meeting with the family before my surgery. This family meeting was not a discussion on where we were going for vacation, but a very sobering serious conversation. Our family was used to meetings. We have a U-shaped kitchen booth where all the decisions were made. It was made and designed in the forties and has been the meeting table in our house. We ate at the table, played games on that table and had long personal conversations sitting around that table. In fact our house has been in our family for over forty years. My dad sold the house shortly after my brother, Dave, was killed in an automobile accident on his way back to college in Kentucky. When I returned to Fremont from California twenty years later, the house was for sale. I took the kids through the house just to show them where daddy lived as a boy. It was in such poor shape it almost made me cry. The house used to be so beautiful and knew the potential if fixed up correctly. I bought the house and remodeled it better than it was when we lived there. I wish we were sitting at that table now to discuss our vacation rather than meeting in the hospital to discuss my health concerns.

I had been trying to make it light conversation most of the time but there was a sense of urgency they recognized in both my voice and actions. I could see the fear of uncertainty in their eyes. A week ago we were looking at potential new homes for Sarah and today we are making life changing decisions. It was an eye opening experience for each of us but particularly for me. We were discussing various items but my mind kept wandering to each of children. I saw their childhood in each of them flash before me and realized how fortunate we were to never have any major issues with any of them. We were so fortunate to have wonderful kids who grew up to be even more beautiful adults. I began to appreciate them even more as I looked from face to face. Parents know that each child has their own unique personality. They all are so different yet I loved each of them equally. They understood the need for the meeting. I wanted them to know exactly what was happening and have a clear understanding of the expectations.

We all had the utmost confidence in Dr. Hermann Kessler who was assigned to my case. He was very impressive in colorectal surgery and was recently recruited by the Cleveland Clinic from his native country of Germany. He spoke seven languages but was very fluent in English. He made us feel this was going to be a routine surgery. We kept our conversation very surface as no one wanted to discuss the seriousness of the upcoming surgery. The Cleveland Clinic is a world renowned facility where people come from everywhere requesting counsel from the very same surgeons getting ready to perform their expertise on me. We were in the right place to get me well again. Maybe this was going to be a small hiccup as we didn't know much about cancer in general even though it was all around us. I don't know if it was my defense mechanism, a lack of empathy, or my eternal optimism but I was not too worried. I had no idea what was going to happen going forward.

This was a common problem I found among most cancer patients. No one really knows what to expect. We had to rely on strangers as everything was moving at light speed. There is no time to think about the alternatives as surgeons are very direct and on a schedule regarding the test required to proceed. If you are removed from this whirlwind you have the luxury to step back and think of all the alternative medicines and procedures around the world. If you are the one involved, you just want to get well. You rely on the expertise and direction from the surgeons. Surgery was eminent, there was no getting around it. The tumor was large and located in my lower ascending colon. I asked Dr. Kessler how this could have happened as I always took the precautions arranging a colonoscopy on the recommended schedule. In fact, I had a colonoscopy less than two years earlier. He said there is no way to be accurate but could only suggest the physician did not perform a full colonoscopy. It was very difficult and more risky to scope all the way into the bottom of the ascending colon. It was customary for a physician not to take the risk if the rest of the colon looked normal. He surmised the physician looked at my colon, did not see any polyps and made the decision not to complete the scope. If he would have taken the risk, he could have cut away what was then just a polyp. This decision escalated into my emergency today. There were so many instances similar to mine that the law was changed. It is now a mandate that the physician has to make a full colonoscopy and take a picture of the bottom of the ascending colon. This offers proof a full scope was performed. I thought how ironic as I was counting on the expertise of the surgeons to remove the tumor as much as I counted on the expertise of the physician performing the colonoscopy.

3

GETTING READY FOR SURGERY

Surgery was scheduled for early Thursday morning in case they needed additional time. The surgeon was hoping to perform laparoscopic surgery to reduce the scar volume and promote a quicker recover. They were to remove the tumor, cut a portion of the colon and put me on the path to recover. At least this was the thought process going into the operating room. My family was there getting the last few words of encouragement and instructions from the surgeon. He was very confident which is just what we all needed at this acute time of uncertainty. There was that elephant in the room which nobody seemed to want to discuss. We needed to have a family meeting prior to the surgery. I met with the four kids in a separate area for a family discussion just off the nurses' station. We had to discuss the obvious short term future if things didn't go as planned. I tried to stay very positive but firm with our conversation. We have always been extremely open with our conversation and thoughts. When I first started dating Patti, she was very surprised at the openness we shared. The kids would come home from a date and share their thoughts and ask for guidance on situations that may have arose on the dates. This openness didn't just start, we embraced this when they were toddlers. I tried to answer all their "why" questions and would offer a few thoughts to ponder on their own. If they had a question I would answer openly with an adult tone to reinforce their right to ask any question they would think to ask. However, we were now discussing my mortality and how it will affect them. This was new territory for all of us. It should not have surprised me but the questions were direct and poignant. We needed to deal with our fears but realize there was nothing we could not handle or overcome. We had many family struggles which we had to develop through. Each family has their own set of struggles but how you view them is how you overcome them. If you allow the struggle to engulf you, it will appear insurmountable. You can view it as another challenge and systematically break it down to what is reality and what is perceived. Some things you cannot control, don't dwell on those. Breakdown the issues which are real and controllable. We always looked at the glass half full which proved important at this time. We discussed the possibility of death but concentrated on the challenges going forward after surgery. This was not routine surgery, nor a routine illness. The challenges were not going to be routine either.

A few snags happened along the way during surgery. There was first, the size of the tumor. It was the size of a softball so they could not perform the laparoscopic surgery as planned and had to resort to the old large cut on the belly surgery. Everything else went smooth as they did not even have to introduce an ileostomy. I was relieved as I knew the challenges of having a temporary ileostomy. The first awareness I had was looking at the ceiling in recovery.

Secretly I was happy to be alive. I had no idea what time it was, I looked around and the nurses were busy but quickly noticed I opened my eyes. They reassured me the surgery went well and once my vital signs were normal I could see my family. What a relief, I felt for the bag at my side and there was none so knew the surgery was a success. I became aware of my thirst and asked for a drink which they refused until I was more stable. They would check my vitals then walk away. I needed my family to know I was awake. I asked the nurse to please let me family know I was awake and recovering which they assure happened an hour ago. I didn't realize I was coming and going into a sleep in the recovery room. This was all new to me as the only other surgery I had was a ruptured Achilles thirty years earlier. There was no consciousness of the time until I actually found a clock. I was in recovery for hours before they finally allowed Patti to visit me. It was late at night and Patti and Sarah had been waiting all day with no updates. The wait continued into the evening and the hospital staff eventually moved them to another waiting area. They were sure it was going to be bad news as the surgery was lasting more than ten hours. The surgery was not scheduled to be this long. It was our first experience and we didn't understand there was hospital time and then there is surgeon time. They don't always coincide. What a sight of joy when Patti came around the curtain with that big infectious smile. She and Sarah looked tired but gave me all the good news of the surgery. Dr. Kessler felt he got all the cancer and only three of the forty nine lymph nodes had any signs of cancer. Even those which were cancerous were the closest to the tumor, as the others showed no signs of intrusion. The tumor itself was very unusual as Dr. Kessler explained it actually walled itself off from the rest of the body. The tumor grew inside the colon and said I was very fortunate to discover it when we did. It would have closed in about two weeks. He explained I would have been dead before I hit the ground. He told me the size of the tumor was one of the largest ever removed at the Cleveland Clinic and would definitely make the journal. I was barely recovering from the surgery but looked squarely into his eyes and said, "It will be a heck of a lot more impressive for the journal if the patient lives". He was tired from the long surgery but he laughed as hard as anyone. He knew this patient was going to be different. He continued to explain in detail the procedure which Sarah had to reiterate to us in layman's terms. We were so glad to have Sarah as our interpreter throughout the ordeal. Not everyone has a daughter with a Masters in nursing by their side, so I suggest having a notebook for every appointment or discussion with the doctors.

I was back in my room that evening with the rest of the family anxious to see me. I could tell the signs of relief on their faces and knew we may have dodged a big bullet. The night was my night to rest but the challenges were addressed early the next morning. Dr. Kessler's group were making their rounds and put up the challenge to walk the halls. We reviewed the surgery and he was optimistic he would be able to get all the cancer. Now came the hard work of walking the halls to get the bowels working again. It was important to get moving to wake the body. My boys were pushing me like I used to push them in sports. I knew it was beneficial to walk as it promoted the movement in the bowels but somewhere along the line the nurse mentioned to them I could not walk too much. They took that literally! They pushed me hard and would not accept that I was not energetic enough to make another trip. Each day they felt I should be walking more, while at the same time it was becoming more difficult for me. To make matters worse, my high school football coach was on the same floor and was walking around like he was strolling in the park. It became increasingly more difficult, and I would perspire and become breathless one trip around the floor. The boys would challenge me saying look at your coach run circles around you, quit being such a pansy. I didn't find out until much later I was not on the colorectal floor and his surgery was much less intrusive. It did not matter as the boys were giving me the challenge. I did continue to walk and push myself, but each time it became more tiring and produced heavy perspiration. Patti got to the point where she was getting concerned at my efforts as the perspiration continually got worse. The nursing staff was not concerned as my vital signs were improving. The only issue was my bowels were not showing signs of life. They couldn't get a sound from the bowels but it still was only days after the surgery. They assured us that sometimes it may take up to a week before the bowels show signs of recovery. I continued to walk the halls with my family at my side every step of the way.

It was getting more difficult and I found myself sweating profusely. The boys made fun of me and pointed to my old football coach but I tried to push on. Patti no longer joined us on our walks as she was very worried. Something was not right, she could feel it and was scoffed at by the boys when she insisted they stop pushing me. We sat around until it was time for them to go home for Thanksgiving. Patti decided to stay with me at the hospital rather than go home with the children. She could use a good night sleep but her instincts told her to stay with me.

4

A NOT SO HAPPY THANKSGIVING

*I*t was the night before Thanksgiving, exactly one week from my surgery when I began to perspire like a faucet. My family encouraged me to keep walking as the nurses prescribed but I knew something was not right. Patti was very concerned when the rest of the family went home for Thanksgiving. They were not as concerned as Patti and promised they would be back the next day for a visit. Patti's instinct to stay the night paid off. It wasn't until about 1:00 AM did the symptoms begin to turn violent. It was becoming more difficult to breathe, and I was losing consciousness. The hospital nurse did my vitals a couple hours earlier and again, was not concerned. Patti would see me suffering and run to the nurse's station to insist she call a doctor only to find her texting or playing games on her phone. I was unable to breath and was holding the top of my bed railings trying to get some room into my lungs to breathe. Patti finally convinced her to call the doctor from another floor around 2:30 AM. When the doctor arrived I could see a look of panic. He barked out some orders and within minutes they stuck a tube down my throat. I instantly puked several large containers of bile. This temporarily relieved my shortness of breath but I knew I was in trouble. The sense of urgency of the doctor made me realize the nurse may have waited too long to finally call him. My body began to settle down and my mind was able to rest with minimal restrictions. I was looking forward to what Dr. Kessler had to say the next morning. Maybe this was a normal reaction. It is not like I had a lot of experience recovering from surgery. It was around 5:30 AM when Dr. Jean Ashburn entered the room advising me she was on call for Dr. Kessler as he just started a week long Thanksgiving vacation back in his German motherland. She informed me an emergency surgery was scheduled for 7:00 AM. I knew my health was in a life threatening situation as no one schedules surgery for Thanksgiving morning unless it was critical. I was relatively calm going into the surgery and tried to be somewhat brave around the family. We all talked calmly but in the back of my mind I was afraid I would not survive the surgery. I was not being positive in my own mind. My thoughts were going a mile a minute while the family and friends gathered. They were all sharing in small talk conversation. I was laying on my bed waiting for them to take me to surgery. I was staring at the ceiling, this was bad and I knew it. I tried not to cry when saying good bye to the kids and Patti. I scoffed it off by being my normal jovial self. I made the goodbyes sound like I was going to the market for a loaf of bread. I tried not to show the fear that I was experiencing behind the mask. The next scenario was like a scene from a movie, there was no time for an orderly to push me to the operating room, everything was moving very fast. The intern quickly came into my room getting me ready for the trip. He was the one who would take me down to the operating room. He pushed my bed out of the room and tried to move rapidly to the elevator. The cursory goodbyes were distant as he quickly moved through the hall. We went past the nurse's station and I noticed hardly anyone at the desks. The hallways were dimly lit as it was early morning and Thanksgiving at that. He was on his cell phone arguing with someone on the other end, there was not time for another scan. We descended down the floors in the elevator, when the doors opened the hall was strangely absent of light. I was watching the ceiling tiles as he quickly picked up the pace down the dark, deserted halls one might expect on Thanksgiving morning. The halls nor any of the rooms were being used, there were no sounds of anyone in the distance. I could hear Patti walking as fast as she could behind the bed as we were be whisked down the dark, empty hallways to the OR. The intern started saying "stay with me, stay with me". I thought to myself, so this is what it is like to die. I was relieved as I was not in much pain and thought dying is not as bad as I always assumed; I was not in pain but I was just going to fade away. My eyes turned again toward the ceiling tiles swiftly passing as the intern was hurrying faster to the operating room. My thoughts were interrupted by Patti responding "No, you are not going to lose me, I am right here". I started laughing to myself as I realized he was talking to her, not me. Maybe I was overreacting and should not take everything so seriously. I was just starting to convince myself to relax when my mind drifted back to reality as the fear came over me again. I realized this was more than a little serious as it was Thanksgiving morning with a skeleton crew at the Cleveland Clinic yet I was being rushed into surgery. My main surgeon was vacationing in Europe and I was being rushed to surgery where a stranger was going to operate. This was not a perfect scenario. The seriousness kept rushing into my head and I became sad as I thought I may not be there for my grandchildren, my children or my wife.

The kids finally got to the point in their life where I could be an adult friend. I felt we did our job as we were so proud of the adults they had become. It was our time now to enjoy the fruits of our labor. They not only were our children, the kids were our friends. We enjoyed the same things and they liked being around us as much as we liked being around them. We enjoyed nights out at our favorite restaurants, football games and a good movie at the house. It made me very sad while being wheeled down the dark halls that it may all be over. I loved my family very much at every stage of my life. This was another stage to enjoy. I was reflecting on our relationship when a loud bang brought me back to the moment. I immediately realized I busted through the doors into the bright lights of the operating room. It was so white and sterile, the lights were bright and everyone was already there waiting for me. Dr. Ashburn was standing next to the table ready to start. She had the perfect eyes of reassurance but I couldn't help blurt out, "I am counting on you to save my life". Her eyes changed to a very serious glaze, "I will" is all she said. The room got fuzzy as the mask come down on my face. It is amazing how helpless you feel at that moment. Most people are secretly fearful of any surgery and your mortality becomes acutely focused when you are having even the most minor surgery. I really didn't get to say a real good-bye to everyone as I was trying to be so strong. I was trying to keep a secret which everyone knew, this was a life or death situation. In that blink of an eye between the time the mask hit my face and my mind stopped thinking was eternity. I thought of all the things I may miss by letting go during this surgery. I had too much to live for, I was just enjoying our retirement and the children were just beginning to make their lives with their own families. I had to live!

I didn't know it at the time but I look back and can point to this exact moment when I began to realize how blessed I was. I had been concentrating on everything I was going through but did not step back and take myself out of the equation. I wanted to live, but why? No one is truly excited about the concept of death, but I had this dogmatic will to live. I started to put things into perspective which I had never done before. Of course I loved my family and enjoyed life but it was at this very brief moment I became aware how wonderful life is. They say your life passes before your eyes, it didn't for me, I was looking at all the reasons to live. I loved my wife, my family and friends but also thought of strolling through the county fair and seeing my neighbors. I thought about that quiet spot where we get a cup of coffee and watch the people go by. The Sunday drives with no particular place to go but enjoying the free time and soft conversations. In that brief drop of the mask, I knew I was a blessed man.

My desire to be with my family along with the magnificent skill of the surgeon allowed me to survive the surgery. After surgery, Dr. Ashburn came into the room and told the family they were fortunate to have such a stoic man for a father. Most people would have not survived. She had to remove my ascending colon and half of my transcending colon. She attached a stoma to better relieve the pressure from the remaining colon. It had to be done to save my life. I did not want a stoma or an ostomy bag but I knew it was necessary and thanked her for saving my life. I apologized for my last response before going under in the operating room. I told her it was a terrible burden I put on her if I would not have survived. I asked her if she thought I would have survived going into the surgery. She told me she thought I may survive the surgery but would have never recovered afterwards. I guess I knew it was serious but her statement really hit home. I was lucky to survive that ordeal. It turned out there was a leak in my colon as the bile was filling my insides. I went totally septic in my inner cavity. Almost no organ was untouched. I was not out of danger yet. I was told less than eight percent survive a serious septic poisoning. This was no joke, I was in for the fight of my life. I was totally out of reality for several days but at one point, I opened my eyes and was very conscious of my condition and surroundings. I looked squarely into Patti's eyes and said "The only reason I am here is because of prayer." I did not have a vision or see a light at the end of a tunnel, I just knew that prayer got me through this near death experience. I turned my head back looked at the ceiling and went back under.

The time in ICU was a time of either total blank or hallucinations. I was fairly drugged up but can remember watching Patti sitting on the ceiling and had to remind myself it is probably not possible and may be hallucinating. It was pretty much that way for the next ten days. One night they came in for my vitals and I saw a bus parked in the corner of my room. I was looking at the bus through a window and was watching this all from my ceiling. Once the medication began to wear off I realized it was the nurse's mobile station which she had left in my room. The mind is a funny piece of apparatus. Once I became more aware of my surrounds I began watching through my hospital window a large black woman standing against the outside hospital wall dressed in long black topcoat. She had a beautiful large black hat tilted slightly on her head and was bracing herself against the wall of the hospital. I rang for the nurse as it was unusually cold for November and felt someone should help this lady. She assured me she would have someone give her immediate attention. I continued to check on her through my window. My heart was saddened as no one made an effort to help her and she could no longer move. I rang the nurse again telling her about the woman in need. She looked at me and said Mr. Rhodes that is an exhaust pipe you are seeing so just relax we have everything under control. Everything made perfect sense to me but I knew it made no sense at all.

While in ICU, I was always acutely aware of this ultimate desire to live, coupled with the fear of dying. I wanted to be there for my family, see my grandchildren grow and wishing everything would just go back to normal. I was introduced to my new normal within hours of recovery. There was a bag attached to me with gauze covering most of my front side. There were tubes coming out from all sides of me. I tried to count them and got to seven and quit. It took everything I had to concentrate on just the easiest of tasks. There were so many drains and tubes I could not tell where they were attached. I really couldn't move as the nurses would come and go doing their job but never really leaving my eyesight. I had an oxygen mask and was very grateful for it as I really didn't think I could breathe without the help. I was scared, confused and uncertain of what was to come. My mind was going a mile a minute but hardly working at all. I was aware of my surroundings but nothing was computing. It was a very bleak time in my recovery but I was settling in to being referred to bed 50B by the hospital staff. They are all very sweet but they see so much daily they cannot afford to get close emotionally. I understood completely. The staff in ICU does not want to make it too easy on the visitors. There were two uncomfortable metal folding chairs for any guests as they really don't encourage visitors to stay long. They have a job to do and guests and family make it harder for them to get the patient on the road to recovery. Patti was not going to leave my side for very long, especially after the septic incident. If she put her head down the nurses would ask her to leave. She eventually relented enough to go to another floor to put two chairs together or find an empty window sill to get some sleep. Her shower consisted of a towel on the floor and using a washcloth to clean herself. ICU was not made for the comfort of guest, it was all about making the patient well enough to move to another room in the hospital.

5

ON THE ROAD TO RECOVERY

*E*ventually the kids had to get back to their jobs and families leaving Patti and I to fight the fight. I know the kids would get upset when they would want to Facetime with me but I asked Patti to tell them I was just not up to it. It was so hard to explain to your children that I was fighting to stay alive and was using most of my energy just to stay awake. I had no more energy for small talk or facetiming even with the ones I loved the most. The doctors put it best when they said this was my time to fight and nothing else matters at this point. It didn't make it any easier on Patti or me that she was receiving phone calls from David's mother-in- law chastising Patti for not allowing our son to talk with his father. This phone call was made just moments after Patti overheard the nurses say the patient in bed 50B would probably not make it through the day as my organs were shutting down. I was trying to breath and stay conscious while she thought I should be facetiming her son-in-law. Thank goodness Nathan was at the hospital and helped handle the situation. The lesson learned is to assign one family member to be the sounding board regarding the information flow. These times are overwhelming to everyone but no one more so than the patient or the spouse. Everyone means well but most are not conscious of their actions or statements.

I was going in and out but was very conscious of the clock in the room. I felt if I fell asleep I would not wake up. I knew what time the clock said, but I didn't know if it was AM or PM. The only way I could tell was by the amount of activity on the floor, but sometimes even that was hard to tell in an ICU unit. There are no windows or lounge chairs for a visitor to get comfy. The one objective is to get the patient downgraded to a room and visitor's feelings were not taken into consideration. The Cleveland Clinic is a well-oiled machine with the most world renowned physicians, but it was ICU nurses who saved my life. I may be exaggerating a little but I would swear there were two nurses for every patient. At least it felt that way to me. They would patiently ensure every detail was completed to perfection with care. Each nurse made me feel like they were there for me and would do anything possible to guarantee my survival.

One of our many blessings was our caseworker from Anthem. She happened to call to introduce herself right after Patti was kicked out of the ICU after the nurses discovered she heard them mention I was not going to make it through the day. Patti was not supposed to be in the room at the shift change but she was behind the curtain when the nurse gave the oncoming nurse the update. They heard her gasp and quickly told her she was not supposed to be there. As soon as she walked out, she received the call from Dave's mother-in-law, and then a call from our Anthem caseworker, Natalie Eubanks. She introduced herself and explained to Patti that anything she would need, to call her personally. Patti broke down crying telling her the situation. She was so kind and compassionate. She continued to work with us through the rest of our journey. It did not take long for her to become part of our family.

Before our initial surgery the nurses told us to be sure to pack everything as we would not be coming back to the same room. Patti and the kids packed everything we had into the car as we didn't know which room we would be going to. We had no idea there would be so many detours. When I finished ICU they finally got to empty the car and make the room more personal. My pictures, flowers and most important to me, my door sign which Sarah made was back on the door. I had no idea this was just the beginning of the road ahead. The marathon comparison was starting to resonate within me. Almost immediately the nurse wanted me to get out of bed. I had no strength and fear came over me trying to reach the chair next to the bed. I didn't know how weak I had become. It took everything I had to get to the chair. The chair was right next to the bed and I was totally spent trying to reach the chair. I had to rest and had no idea how I was going to make it back to bed. It was such a daunting task and I had to work to get the courage to make the trip back to bed. They next encouraged me to sit on the chair and eat my liquid dinner. It was too much, I had to get back to bed. The bed became my refuge. The evening nurse came in proclaiming I was going to get out of the room and walk the halls. I was a wrestler in high school and college so I always had a lot of tenacity, but this was too much. I was scared to take on the challenge. The next morning she put a chair in the middle of the room and that was to be my new challenge. It took everything in my mind to muster the courage and energy to make it the five steps to the chair. I had to rest in the chair as I was afraid I would not be able to make it back to my bed. It was a very horrifying time for me realizing how far I had slipped. I had no strength but even less courage to face the fight. I was afraid to fall asleep at night as I thought if I slept I would not wake up. It was terrifying for me. I would watch Patti sleep in the lounge chair they finally brought for her. I think the nurses felt sorry for her sleeping in the window sill in the cold days of December. It was during the night I formalized my plan for recovery. I had to overcome my fear of trying in order to take the steps I needed to recover. It was like an athlete getting ready for the big game. I didn't have the time to fully prepare my brain for the fight ahead. That night I began to emotionally get ready for the next day. I was going to make it to the door and back to bed. I was now emotionally in the game.

It was a struggle, but I knew what I had to do. I mustered all my strength and made it to the door before sitting in the chair. I was ready for the challenge to return. It took so much effort but I finally collapsed into the bed completely exhausted. I made it! I would now reward myself with a day in bed resting. The nurse said great job, we will do it again in an hour. She outperformed any coach I have ever had in sports. She barked commands with such authority I knew I better get ready for the next round in one hour. I hated her and loved her. I knew she was on a mission to get me on the road to recovery. I looked at the clock knowing she would be relieved shortly and I would then be able to rest. They did the rounds with the oncoming nurse and when she came to me, she said push him hard he wants to get out of bed, he just doesn't know it yet. This nurse had one day with me and already had me pegged. She had me walking in the hall and, with Patti's help, was strolling around the nurses' station within a week.

My mouth was always so dry and I was getting tired of Gatorade. I told Dr. Kessler the dietician told me no sweets and nothing to drink but Gatorade. He said that was not his orders and told me I could eat sweets and even drink sweet tea if I wanted. He left the room and Patti was already pulling money from her wallet. I know what you want and will be right back. She came back with a big gulp size cup of McDonald's sweet tea. I started drinking that big cup letting it drip down my chin. It was so refreshing and sweet. I drank the whole cup in one continuous motion. Patti went to get me another one. The second cup I drank more civilized as I wanted to savor the taste of this one. The nurse's aide brought in the evening meal which had a piece of chocolate cake on the tray. I was so looking forward to some normal food while washing it down with my new best friend, the sweet tea. I was feeling normal for an ever so slight moment. I looked at my ostomy bag and it was filling up like a faucet was turned on. We yelled for the nurse but it was too late. The bag burst sending the sweet tea all over the floor. The stoma wouldn't stop as it was still producing fluid at a pace of a bathtub faucet. They had to attach a tube from the stoma into a bucket. It was generating that much fluid. The nurse called the dietician to figure out what went wrong. It did not take her long to find the source. "Who said you can have sweet tea, certainly not me". I was not going to be the fall guy, I quickly through Dr. Kessler under the bus. She made sure the floor nurses served nothing other than Gatorade then glanced at my dinner tray. She quickly grabbed the cake and through it in the trash. I was speechless, first the sweet tea and now my cake. My quick shadow of freedom was thrown in the trash. She explained the sweets produced an irregular effect on my stoma which would have pushed me into dehydration. The body was cleansing itself of all the excess fluids which is what caused the flood from the stoma. It was still well worth it, I had the ever so brief taste of being normal. It gave me that goal I had been missing.

I continued to push myself and be pushed, Patti now had the strength in numbers to tell me what to do. She became the drill sergeant when the nurses were not in the room. My strength was slowly growing. Patti felt more confident in leaving me long enough to go to another floor to get a much needed shower. She kissed me goodbye and said the nurses were going to allow her to actually shower with running water and was going to be gone for about an hour. I thought this would be a great time to surprise her and shave for the first time in a month. I was still unable to stand for long periods of time so I asked the nurse for a chair so I could sit while I shaved. I looked in the mirror and realized I had a short beard. I only had a straight razor and knew this was going to take some time. I would concentrate on one area at a time and then move to the next area until I was cleanly shaved. I worked on my right cheek but took more than a couple swipes to get the coarse beard which had grown over time. I must have taken fifteen swipes at the same area on my right cheek. Finally there was skin but I became so exhausted I needed to stop. I looked at the mirror and saw a big hole in my beard but also noticed my eyebrows have grown to an Andy Rooney look-a-like. They were longer than my eyelashes. I needed to trim them as I wanted to feel more normal. I only had my razor so used the blade to trim them a little. I now had several spaces of skin separating the rest of my eyebrow. I was overcome with exhaustion and had to go back to bed.

Patti walked in several moments later and gasped, "What happened to you?". She was laughing hysterically and could barely tell me what I did. I had a hole in my beard in my right cheek and shaved my left eyebrow almost completely off. I was now ready for my Friday night visitors.

The episode did make me realize how weak I still was and how far I needed to go. In between my daily walks the nurses would come in as a group and work on changing drains and various bandages. At one point, they motioned to Patti for help as they said she would need to continue to do this when we got home. They were standing around my bed looking at my midsection. Patti walked to their side, looked where they were looking and almost passed out. They instantly got her a chair and said she would get used to it. I asked what the issue was as I had no idea there was anything outside of the drains. They produced a mirror and I was able to see this massive hole in my stomach area. They had to open my midsection and leave it open to remedy the remains of being septic. It was an open hole and could see as deep as my intestines but with a very thin layer of skin covering the bottom of the hole. They said I needed to heal from the inside out and it may take up to one year. This area would need to be packed with special gauze bandages and changed two to three times per day to avoid infection. I only knew I had a large bandage covering my midsection but had no idea what was on the other side. It was interesting looking at it and would have been a nice day in science class but this was my stomach. It scared both of us when we thought how easily I could have another infection. Patti took it upon herself to learn how to pack the hole without making me jerk with pain. The nurses used long Q-tips to adjust the bandages into place, but would sometimes touch my insides. My body would react with a large jerk as it felt like someone was poking my insides with a knife. She hated to watch the ordeal and vowed to take her time adjusting the gauze and positioning them to soak up the infection. She would continue to change my packing three times per day until my subsequent surgery to have my ostomy reversal which would be nine months later. The doctors were getting us ready for discharge. I had seven drains which Patti had to learn to monitor, an open wound and an ostomy bag. We were nervous to be released and were discussing the issues with the doctor when one of the drains popped out of the hole in my side, shooting across the floor. Patti started crying saying she would not be able to give me the proper care. From that moment, Patti would take the time to re-pack the open wound three times each and every day. She became organized with the drains, the discharge and its monitoring. The doctor tried to convince her to repack the wound once per day to make it easier on her. She said it was much easier to change the bandages an extra time or two rather than see me go through another infection. Patti felt confident to make the next step away from the hospital to a rehabilitation center.

PICTURES

This sign made by Sarah was posted on every one of my hospital rooms.

My friend Santa visiting me at the rehabilitation facility.

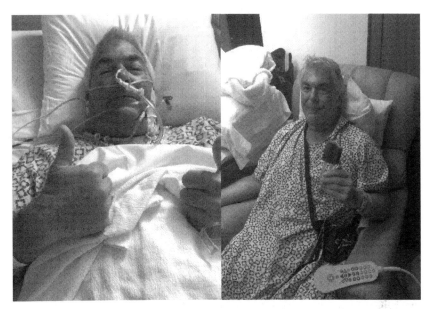

Above Left: On the road to recovery! Above Right: Enjoying my fluid treat on the infamous lounge chair. Notice how close it is to the bed but early in recovery felt so far away.

My sister, Cheryl, visiting me at the Cleveland Clinic.

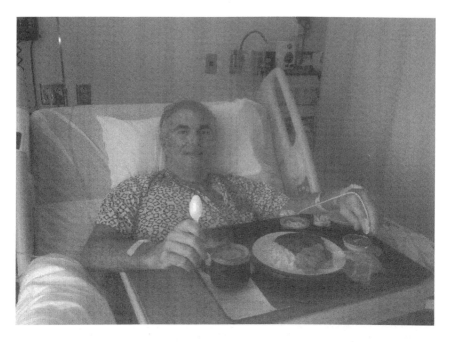

My first solid meal was a memorable event, even if the food was not so memorable.

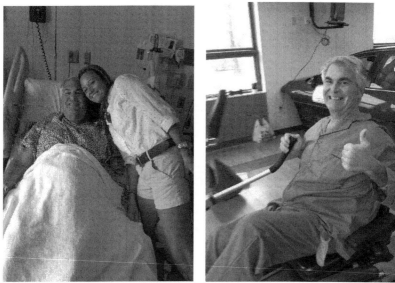

Above Left: Sarah on one of her frequent visits. Above Right: Working hard at the rehabilitation center. Notice the drain poking from under the pajamas.

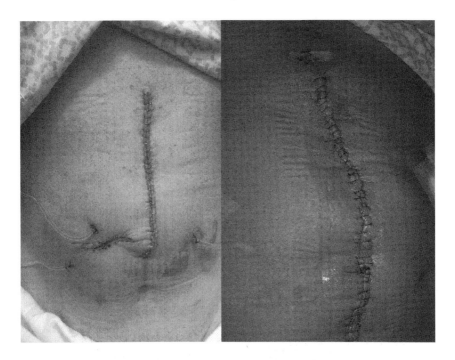

Above Left: Photo taken after my ostomy reversal. Above Right: Dr. Rosenblatt's work of art.

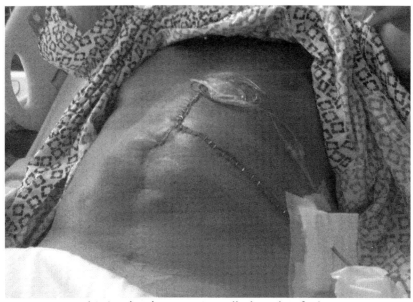

This is why the surgeon called me beefcake.

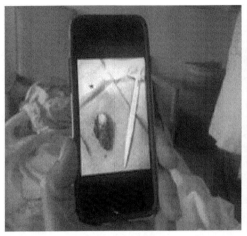 

Above Left: Picture of Dr. Berber's phone which he took of the removed section of the Vena cava. Above Right: Actual photo of the by-pass team reconnecting the vena cava during Dr. Berber's surgery.

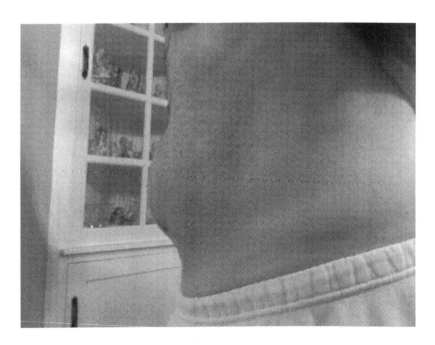

The first hernia showing itself after my reconnection surgery.

6

TRYING TO UNDERSTAND REHABILITATION

*I*t was very difficult finding the right rehabilitation hospital as there are many incidentals we never thought about. You have to be sure your insurance is covered at the facility as well as if the facility could handle my needs. It appeared no one in my area was equipped to handle my open wounds and ostomy needs. They lacked the man-power required to facilitate my daily bandage changes. Finally the worker at the clinic was able to find a match as long as Patti would stay and help them on a daily basis to empty drains, repack the open wound and change the ostomy bag. This was an easy concession as Patti was not going anywhere else as long as I was in the hospital.

I was excited to finally get out of the hospital. Well, at least, to another hospital which they called rehabilitation. It was close to my home and would be much easier for the kids to visit. Sarah was helping Patti arrange my room with the ostomy supplies we were given from the Cleveland Clinic. Our nurse walked through the door, and we all realized we were not at the Cleveland Clinic anymore. She had a heavy odor of cigarette smoke and said she was there to help Patti change my open wound. We all noticed she did not wash her hands as she walked through the door. This was a habit we became very accustomed to at the Clinic. Every level of personnel would wash their hands as they entered and when they left. It was a habit we quickly adopted. Patti and Sarah in unison said you are not touching anyone until you wash your hands. She said she washed them down the hall and it was okay. She was instructed sternly by the two woman I love the most, she was to wash her hands when she entered the room where we could see it was done, before she performed any duties. We worked too hard to avoid infections and we were not going to let our guard down at this point. I know she was offended at first but did oblige us by always washing her hands as she entered the room thereafter. It was those little things that make the Cleveland Clinic outstanding.

It was a couple days before Christmas and Patti and Sarah were determined to make it as normal as possible. They scheduled a room in the hospital where the kids decorated with our traditional ornaments from home. Sarah was definitely in charge, giving the boys their chores. In the end the place looked much like home with all the decorations and stockings hung by the IV tree with care! Sarah was like me as she loved tradition. We do the same thing every year in the same order. Our decorations are in the same place and we even prepare the same hors d'oeuvres every year. One year Patti suggested we try something different which resulted in an instant mutiny.

True to form for the Rhodes family, northern Ohio was hit with 20-40 degrees below zero wind chill temperatures. This did not deter our family from celebrating Christmas as normal as possible. I became quite emotional as I knew how much effort they made to make it a special time for me. It was a difficult walk to the front of the hospital, right to the end of the hall, to the decorated room. I was still not out of danger and was thinking this may be my last Christmas so I wanted to make it a joyous one. This is my first conscious decision to move forward and try not to complain but I was still holding back the tears. I did not want to be that negative person no one wants to be around, especially at Christmas. It is hard to be positive as you really do have to make a transformation in your mind. I realize negatives are instilled in us daily and to be positive really does take an effort. The more you practice it the easier it becomes. Patti would tell me everyone who visited thought I looked fine and was making a remarkable recovery. I put a positive spin on everything trying to be positive and always smiling. It was just as easy to be nice as it was to be angry with everyone. I was not being naïve or unaware, I was practicing to live my life going forward. However, I had always been one who cried easily. I am that man who cries at the movies. I would still cry even though I have seen the same movie a hundred times. This Christmas was going to be a challenge for me. I was so proud and happy to have everyone there. Everyone, with the exception of Nate as he had to fly Christmas Day as he was still a junior status pilot with Southwest Airlines. The more senior pilots wanted to be home so he was always scheduled to work. The other children made it very special and of course the grandchildren loved it as much as any other time. My old friend, Bobbie Johns, showed up in his Santa Claus suit. Bobbie has been Santa Claus since my kids were little and this is the only Santa my children or the grandchildren ever knew. Bobby was a friend of my older brother and when Patti called and told him our circumstances, he quickly accepted to make the trip. He could have just as easily said no with a built in excuse due to his schedule and the terrible weather. My friends were coming out to support me and I was very grateful to Bobby as he really does look like the real Santa. My grandchildren will see a department store Santa and say out loud that he must be a fake, he doesn't look anything like the real Santa. He is such a great look-a-like that he was named the Big Ten Network Santa Claus. Everything was as normal as it could be. The surroundings were new, and I was in pajamas rather than a suit but the kids, especially Sarah, made it very special for me. Dave even Facetimed Nate so he could be there as well. Nate watched as we painstakingly opened each present one by one. This was a tradition we all loved. If someone opened a present, the giver would discuss why they thought of that person for that present. The receiver would put their present in their pile in another area and would start over. We cleaned the wrapping paper, put away the ribbon and bows and started with the next one. The room was clean of paper and the next present was opened as if it was the first. Patti and I actually had most of the presents bought this year which was unusual for us. Sarah and Patti wrapped them and even had some ready for Santa to give to the grandchildren. We made it work under the circumstances. I was grateful as it was as normal as it could possibly be and I escaped the hospital world if just in the other room. I found myself tearing up with each present but I don't think anyone noticed.

The rehabilitation was hard but seemed silly to me. I understand the reasoning of standing and playing the game Candy Land, but it was a bit humbling to me. Bouncing a ball with the therapist seemed like such a waste of time but I understood it was building my stamina and coordination. It was not good for the mind though as I thought this is what I was reduced to. Walking the halls, working on my laptop and making sales calls was my kind of therapy, not Candy Land. I tried to stay positive with the therapist but they knew they were losing me to my real therapy. I finally convinced Patti to bring my laptop to the hospital. That is when my rehabilitation began. I felt more normal doing the things I enjoyed doing. I could send my emails, answer questions and get back into the professional world. My customers were my friends. It didn't start that way when I first started in business. We had no history together and secretly wanted to be like that guy who knew everyone and could name drop the giants of the transportation industry. Over the years a close business relationship developed and without a conscious thought my customers became close friends. I was eager to establish contact again. It has been two months and I didn't know if they were aware of my diagnosis and probably wondering where I have been. The worries were unfounded as so many cards and letters were sent but left unopened until I could read and digest them. It was overwhelming as the love and true heartfelt concern was shown in each message. Once I opened my emails, it was apparent my customers were aware. There were so many messages with the bottom line always offering me best wishes and letting me know their prayers would continue.

I have never been a big card sender, but I now realized how a little card can mean so much to a person isolated in a hospital bed. A few moments out of the day to send a card was so hard for me to do. You have to find a card, write a little message and then send it seemed like such an undaunted task. I never saw the effect at the other end until it was me. Now we buy cards by the boxes and send as many and as often as possible to my friends and general acquaintances. I know the effect of a brief message just saying I am thinking of you.

I had my first follow up appointment with the Cleveland Clinic while still a patient at the rehabilitation center. We had to make the ninety mile each way trip in a snow storm with subzero temperatures. Patti was nervous to make the trip by herself in case something happened. She was not used to driving in the Cleveland traffic let alone in a snow storm with a passenger who was not going to be much help. Our dear friend, Cindi Auxter, must have heard of the situation. She called Patti and told her she was driving us to our appointment in her SUV. Cindi was not asking to drive us, she was telling Patti she was driving us. There was no room for Patti to be polite and say no. It was such a welcomed offer. Cindi owns a very cute gift store in our hometown. It is her pride and joy as she has collectables from around the world. Her husband, Tom, was a big burly man and cute collectables was not in his vocabulary. Tom was in Florida at the time when Cindi told him of her plan to drive us. He scheduled to have the car serviced, cleaned and ready for the trip to Cleveland all from his condo in Florida.

It was a blistering winter morning when Cindi pulled up for our trip to Cleveland. We laughed as we felt strength in numbers but we consisted of an invalid and two women not over five feet or weighing a hundred pounds. Cindi wrapped me in a huge blanket to keep me warm for the trip. I realized as we were driving, this was the first I had been out since I entered the hospital in November. I was transported to the rehabilitation center in an ambulance so I could not see a thing. The snow was blowing sideways and the roads were empty as it was early morning and the weather was not conducive for a leisure drive. We drove past the frozen water of Lake Erie and the snow covered fields of cut corn. We chatted the whole trip but my mind was wandering. So much has happened since my last drive to Cleveland. We were planning on a four or five day stay at the hospital. Here we are over two months later with so much change. Our world has turned around on us in seemingly a flash of a second. We had so many expectations for retirement since both of us were so healthy and active. We have all the reasons to feel sorry for ourselves. It suddenly hit me that I had to snap out of these thoughts of depression. I needed to stay positive and live my life. I do understand how people get emotionally withdrawn during their bout with cancer. It is too easy to dwell on the negatives. No one would blame them but life goes on and I do too!

We arrived at the clinic and Patti got me a wheel chair. I didn't think about it but there was no way I could make the walk to the elevators, up to the reception desk and down the hall to the waiting room. I knew this but was not prepared to be pushed around in a wheel chair. I now understood the need for therapy, for standing while playing candy land or bouncing a ball with the therapist. I had to regain my strength. It was not going to just come back, I had to push myself. It was a new found revelation for me. I was waiting around to get healed rather than working to heal myself. Things were going to be different when I got back to the rehabilitation center.

My first visit was uneventful but lengthy. Patti had a ritual of giving Dr. Kessler a big hug every time he would enter the room. This began when he told her I survived the first surgery. It took so long, her mind was convinced I did not make it through the surgery. When he walked through the door with a smile, her first instinct was to give him a big hug. She would give him a hug every time he did his daily rounds in the hospital. I jokingly told her she may want to stop with the hugs as I thought he was single and may let me just pass if he thought she was available. He always produced a big smile and the interns were all amused at her throwing her arms around this otherwise stern man.

Dr. Kessler thought I was recovering well and congratulated Patti on the job she was doing with my open wound. She continued to change the packing three times per day on her own. The wound showed no signs of infection. This was a little surprising to them since it was an actual open wound and very susceptible to infections. Hospitals are the easiest place to get an infection and have not left a hospital environment since the surgery. Patti was doing a remarkable job. They decided to change my ostomy bag and discovered the product they were using at the rehabilitation center was equivalent to a concrete compound to attach my stoma and the bag. The nurse spent over an hour picking this compound out of my stoma. It was painful as she had to take tweezers to pull this compound away from raw skin. She showed Patti what the center was doing wrong so it would not be repeated. She offered a few other tips when changing the bag. I was unique when it comes to the ostomy bag as I also had the wound. There was less than an inch between the edge of the open wound and the circle of the stoma. When attaching the bag to my skin, the adhesive area had to be trimmed to fit around the wound. This resulted in my bag needing to be changed more often than normal patients.

We finally finished and found Cindi resting in a chair. She sat patiently waiting for us and welcomed us with a big smile. This is Cindi Auxter and why we remain such good friends. We always found ourselves attracted to positive people but even more now. Tom and Cindi had a condo close to ours in Florida and became even closer friends as time went on. Ironically Tom was diagnosed with pancreatic cancer several years later and I was able to be there for him during that difficult time.

When we returned to the rehabilitation center we were all tired and said our goodbyes. Patti and I rested but reviewed our notes from the appointment as we learned so much about changing the ostomy. Things were going to be different as we knew we had to do things on our own. I had to take a bigger part in my own rehabilitation. I had been passive as I did not see the benefit in the treatment. I knew I had to drive myself harder if I didn't want to be pushed around in a wheel chair in the future.

7

FINALLY, HOME

*I*t was so good to be home. The mattress we bought the day before I went to the hospital was still new with that new mattress smell. Oh, it was good to be home! Nothing had changed. The house looked the same, as clean as the day we left it two months prior. I am not sure what I expected but I somehow realized life just goes on. Nothing stops, just because you are not there. It was a sobering thought at first but I didn't want my mind to wander too far, I was just glad to be home! Everything was the same, only different. I couldn't help but think of the book: The Tale of Two Cities. This was the best of times but the worst of times. I certainly have changed. Physically, I was not the same man who left for appendix surgery in November, but I was changed spiritually, as well. I valued the little things and no longer worried about things I could not control. It was a gift I wished I had received much earlier in life, but I appreciated having this new focus now. Maybe I would change as I matured anyway but either way cancer gave me a gift I was not going to let go to waste.

I tested my diet with Chinese food, rice and a great dessert. All the things I could not get on the hospital menu. My appetite was still strong, as I have not started the most challenging part of my journey yet. I knew they wanted to start chemo as quickly as possible. My two months in the hospital after the diagnosis put the treatment behind schedule. I came home on a Friday and had to have my port installed the following Wednesday so I could begin chemo on Monday. Another surgery! The nurses told me this would be very easy, and I would not feel a thing and by morning could regain my normal lifestyle. They lied. I woke up, pushed myself to a sitting position and almost fell off the bed. It was not quite as easy as they described as my left side, where the port was installed, was terribly sore. It went away after a couple days but I was looking forward to a small reprieve from pain before I started my chemo regiment. I was ready to get this treatment behind me as I was told it was totally precautionary. The surgeon was confident he got all the cancer. My mind was racing as I just wanted to finish this portion and was a little scared the treatment was going to be worse than the cancer. I had two people diagnosed about the same time, and they were just starting their chemo treatment. One was a mother of one of our closest friends. She was one of those people they should mold grandmothers around. Always upbeat, full of life and compliments and easy to laugh. I was home only a couple days and found she passed away from complications of her chemotherapy. This was devastating news to me. I thought chemo cured people not make them worse. What was I getting myself into? Maybe I should just pass this chemo treatment since it was just precautionary anyway. I convinced myself her age and the fact she was going to another center other than the Cleveland Clinic gave me the courage to forge ahead. Then another friend was between her second and third treatment at the Cleveland Clinic and was having a few issues. She had to have surgery and died during the procedure. I was at a loss for words. This fight was for real and there were many more things to be weary of besides just the cancer. The doctor's words echoed in my mind. He told me I would be in for the fight of my life and to always remember it was a marathon not a sprint. He was right! My eyes were opened, this was not going to be a cake walk. I became aware of the number of people who died from complications from the treatment as much as the disease itself. I began to read the books everyone gave me regarding chemotherapy, cancer and positive thinking. I was determined to win. I was going to beat this thing. I told Patti that cancer may take my life but it was no longer going to take a day away from me. I would use that phrase many times during my fight with cancer. That was how I was going to win. I felt I no longer had control whether I was going to die, but I did have control over living. It was at that time I made the decision to be positive, live life daily as I really did not know how long I was going to live. This rings true in everyone's life as so many people lose their life daily without an illness or warning. I had this chance to re-dedicate myself to truly living. I have always packed a lot of living into a routine day, but this disease was not going to keep me down. I was going to live my life as normal as possible on a daily basis. I had to look at each day as a new beginning and treat each day independently of any other day. I needed to get through that day, the best I could with the most energy I could. I no longer worried about yesterday or tomorrow, it was today I was going to make the most of.

I was told people would say stupid but well intentioned things when they would greet me after my hospitalization. Thank them, laugh at the statements inside, but understand they had good meanings. That I could deal with but I had no idea visitors would not understand how tired I would get. I loved the visits but it was very difficult to maintain a conversation very long. There were some guests who just didn't understand the toll a visit may take on the patient. I finally realized I just had to say I was tired and needed a nap and found everyone was understanding to that phrase. Don't ever hesitate to be upfront with your visitors as their intentions are well meaning and they want only the best for your recovery. Be prepared for some interesting well wishes. We had a very close friend stop to offer a casserole and stayed to visit for a while. Her conversation was well intended as she told me I would beat cancer as I was a tough person. She then went on to tell us how her sister-in-law battled colon cancer and died very rapidly. She also told us how strong willed her mother was and fought very hard but passed away from cancer within a year. Very uplifting information to share when I just got home from the hospital. Good intentions, just not very well thought through words. I have been in that position and I often was at a loss for words, it is very difficult to put yourself in their position. Very few people have a great command of the English language and know the appropriate thing to say. As a visitor, just be yourself and don't worry about the gorilla in the room. Speak open, as long as it is with love. It will be well received. As a patient, I just wanted to have a conversation, any conversation, whether it was about the cancer or the local gossip. After all, this was just a minor setback for me. Everything was good as the surgeon said he surgically removed the cancer and my chemotherapy was merely cautionary.

When we finally met with Dr. Fanning, my oncologist, he told me there was more than a good chance the surgeon did not get all the cancer cells during surgery. He said surgeons can afford to be optimistic, oncologist cannot. He explained there are rogue, microscopic cells undetected by the surgeons eyes and can hide for months until they rear themselves in a PTSCAN. The chemotherapy would take care of many of these rogue cells but it had to be aggressive. If the first round of chemotherapy did not work, my odds of survival would be reduced dramatically. This was a sobering comment as I was told this was just precautionary. I blurted out to him, "What are my chances for survival?" He said thirty percent without blinking an eye. I thought I was through the danger and he said I was at a thirty percent survival chance. I was silent on the ride home and Patti asked what was wrong. I teared up saying I couldn't believe I only have a thirty percent chance for survival. She looked at me and said what are you worried about it is four times better than when I went septic. When I went septic my chance of survival was at eight percent, which I didn't know until much later in my recovery. Dr. Ashburn even told me, she thought I would survive the surgery but never recover and go home. Patti laughed at me loudly and said I thought you were going to always be positive. Where's my Jack! She was right but I still wanted a little time to feel sorry for myself before chemotherapy would get started.

I was proud of myself as I continued to force myself to get out of the house. I was so drained from months in the hospital even the daily activities were very difficult. I could not lift due to the hernias and had no stamina for long walks. I was going to have to set a daily goal. My neighbor who was born in Eastern Europe told me the secret to his longevity was a daily purpose. He and his wife lived past one hundred years old and did their daily chores manually. Their garden and lawn were their passion and was the envy of the neighborhood. They would haul the water by bucket to the back of their lawn rather than use a garden hose. Sam only ate at a restaurant one time and "Mama" never ate outside their home. They ate what they produced in their garden except for a few strips of meat they would eat as a Sunday Barbeque treat. There was a lot to learn from their behavior. Sam would call me over to his yard showing me with pride the diverse flowers and growth in the garden. He always called me Jackie even though I was an adult. He was sitting on his porch sipping his homemade vino one night and called me to come sit for a chat. He said, Jackie, you have to have a purpose. You have to have a reason to get out of bed each morning. He said if you don't have anything to do, make up chores. He told me it may take him a week to paint a door as he would spend one day taking it off the hinges. The next few days he would sand the door and the next few days were spent painting. This gave him almost seven days of work to paint the door. The point was he had a purpose each day to get out of bed. There was a lot of wisdom in his words. I began to make a list of my daily purpose. It became my famous "to do" list. I would write everything down, even the most basic chores. We began to go to our grocery store almost daily. This was uncharacteristic for us but Patti said it was to buy fresh. I knew it was to get me out of the house and walk the aisles. We are fortunate to have the President Rutherford B. Hayes Presidential library in our hometown. The grounds are beautiful with the grass stunningly manicured. There is a half mile blacktopped walking path inside the gate and around the entire facility. We decided to observe my progress by monitoring how long I could walk on the path. It took me a long time to make one time around the circle. It didn't matter as I was pushing myself and getting out of the house. I was emotionally and physically ready for my next step, Chemotherapy.

8

CHEMOTHERAPY: THE KILLER OF A CURE

The children all bought me books on surviving cancer and what to expect during chemotherapy. There were probably 5-6 books in all. I briefly read through a few but I really didn't want any pre-set thought process going into chemo. The oncologist briefed me on the regiment saying they were going to be very aggressive with my therapy and would give me as much as I could take. It was better to kill as many as possible of the microscopic rogue cells. He continued, if the chemotherapy does not work, the chance of survival greatly diminishes as time goes on. His main suggestions were to stay hydrated and don't let yourself get de-hydrated. As an athlete, dehydrated had a completely different meaning than when you are dealing with cancer. I had no idea there was little difference between your reaction to chemotherapy and dehydration. I was soon to discover the differences.

There is little doubt the doctors and nurses have no idea how scared, confused and unsure of yourself on the first day of chemo. Since each cancer is different there is little to prepare someone for what is to come. My first day was emotional to say the least. I could hardly speak without tearing up. I had my bag packed with a blanket, reading material and a drink. The first day was going to be a long one as they anticipated at least eight hours of treatment. The nurses really do try to make you feel comfortable to the best of their ability. It is a special conviction to be a nurse at a treatment center, and I welcomed their smiles and encouraging words. They took a lot of time explaining each container's purpose and what the effect of the drug would have on my cancer. Felicia was assigned as my nurse that first treatment. She put my mind at ease as the port was accessed and my first chemo treatment commenced. She was a very special outgoing person and I was glad she was there for my first visit. I was emotional and teared up as she began to tell me the routine. Her eyes were the kind that are always smiling and she gently put her hand on my arm and told me she would be there every step of my first day. I am not sure if she saw my tears as she never let on if she did. Felicia probably has gone through this scenario hundreds of times, but it was my first and I needed her reassurances. The first treatment is when you are the most apprehensive and Felicia was able to put my mind at ease. The nurses at the Sandusky Treatment Center of the Cleveland Clinic are a testimony to their profession. Some are more personable than others, but they were all great individuals. We became friends and came to love their smiles and encouraging words. I felt as if they were truly interested in my comfort. I realized it wasn't just me but they made everyone feel special. Not all treatment centers are equal and I have found these girls are superior to say the least. The clinic is well-served having this group. These girls are emotionally up all the time while seeing death and dying in their patients daily. It is hard to remember they have their own life's tribulations. Lynn is one nurse which

Patti and I became particularly close. We would have long conversations, and she would share many of her own troubles she was having in her life. She was not dwelling on problems, they just came up in conversation. The discussions flowed easily as I think she wanted input from an experienced couple. I could not understand how someone as sweet and pretty as Lynn would have any issues. She was always so upbeat with a constant smile. We would run into Lynn out of the treatment center and found it awkward explaining to our friends how I knew this beautiful blonde. She had to protect my privacy and it was difficult to say she was my chemo nurse. A lot of people didn't even know I was battling cancer. The nurses were all so wonderful I hate to recognize them by name as I know I would leave some out. These women were the best group I have encountered throughout my battle, and were special to me and my road for recovery.

The first treatment moved quickly as Felicia made me comfortable. I even found myself getting hungry. Sarah came to the center to be with us for the first treatment. Patti suggested we get a few sandwiches at the local Subway and have a picnic while getting my treatment. I was really trying to change my eating habits but capitulated gratefully. I was on my third bag of chemo before she returned and was I starving by this time. I was salivating by the time I slowly unwrapped my foot long sandwich. I also liked it loaded with almost everything and felt I was really getting my money's worth with all the toppings. I took that first bite and it was heaven. I recognized that so familiar taste on my palate. I took that big second bite known through the family as a large Papack bite. My bites are so big I can eat a normal hamburger in four attacks of the bun. There was something different about the taste of this sandwich on my second bite, something very unfamiliar. It tasted very salty, almost metallic tasting. What was happening, I looked at the vegetable toppings to see if they were spoiled. The nurse walked past and must have noticed my confused look with a mouth full of sandwich. She asked if something was wrong and then she explained to me how the chemo changes your taste buds. They under-exaggerated the changes as some food taste totally different as soon as you begin the chemo treatment. My sandwich tasted like all the vegetables were rotten and nothing really tasted good to me after that moment. It is hard to explain to others how I felt because the food all looked good to me but I just didn't like the taste anymore. Everyone says you need to eat, you cannot afford to lose weight. I tried but only certain foods, at no particular time, tasted good. All the other times, I felt nauseated after one bite. The pills do help with the nausea but not with anything tasting better. One particular chemo, oxaliplatin, also caused my body to react to anything cold. I could no longer put ice in my drinks and eventually had to drink everything warm. I once reached in the fridge for eggs and felt like I had a piece of metal in my hands on the coldest February day in Ohio. You have to understand, I like ice. My drinks are filled to the top of the glass with ice before I pour the beverage into this mountain. Now, I could not only not have ice, but the beverages had to be at room temperature. How could cancer take away my favorite past time!

The other side effects began to manifest itself one after another. It was like one side effect didn't want to be overshadowed by the other. The nausea started but they offer two different types of medication to fight. The first one you try to offset the nausea, if it doesn't work you go to the hard stuff. I could never remember which one was to be taken first and the nausea always began when I didn't have my glasses to read the labels. Whoever designed medicine labels must be looking through a magnifying glass anyway. I decided to label them with a big "1" and "2" to make it easier at night. Next came the diarrhea, I didn't need my glasses to know what to do with this side effect.

My oncologist told me not to get dehydrated. That means nothing to the average patient. As an athlete, I knew if my mouth became dry to drink water. Not so when on chemo. You drink water every day, all the time. Not Smart Water, not Gatorade, but good old fashion water. You cannot drink too much as one of the leading and most damaging issues I have seen is dehydration. This can lead to so many other long lasting problems. This may tell you to listen to your body. In the beginning, I didn't know what that meant. I had to experience issues then try to rectify to understand what my body was telling me. I always thought being fatigued was just a side effect of the chemo. I didn't know it was a warning sign that you are dehydrated even though you think you are drinking plenty of fluids. If you are getting light headed or severely fatigued, call your physician right away and don't let him tell you it is just the side effect of the chemo. Ask him to do blood work or ask for an IV, it is your right as a patient. You need to be fully aware of what is going on inside you. Equally as important is to know what to do to rectify those issues. Due to my loss of colon, dehydration was a particular problem for me. The colon will absorb many of the fluids into your system. My ability for intake was shortened to a dangerously low level. It is equivalent to a person with chronic diarrhea. If you are battling colon cancer you will need to be aware of your increased vulnerability to severe dehydration.

Review the side effects with your physician and what you can do to avoid them if possible. Many oncologist will tell you the side effects are no big deal and they are bound by law to list every possible scenario. Remember, they are listed because more than one patient had the same effect from taking that drug and you may be in that percentage. You may not, but you have to be prepared and aware if you experience any of them. Do not take these lightly but do understand percentage wise you may not experience most of them.

Ask questions and be proactive. Most oncologists are reacting to what they find but may put off surgery or more testing until the condition manifests itself further. Remember, the earlier you treat the cancer the better chance of a full recovery. This includes any metastasis. No one tells you what to expect both physically and emotionally let alone the full understanding of what chemo really is. It is not a cure but can reduce your cell numbers and size hoping your immune system can take over. It is a deadly poison and my first thought was someday people will look back on chemo the same way we look at using leaches as a cure.

It did not take long for the dehydration to raise its ugly head. Mostly because I really did not know what to look for. As I mentioned I was an athlete with an athlete's mentality of dehydration. I was looking for the obvious signs of dry mouth, not being able to urinate but not the slow decline of energy. I thought that was due to the chemo. My son suggested I drink smart water from the very beginning. I always had a bottle of Smart Water or Gatorade with me. Rest assured the best thing to drink is just plain water. If you remember one thing from this book, remember to drink water when on chemo. The doctors even underestimate how much you should drink. The best rule of thumb is to drink as much as you can every single day. Do not skip a day as it is hard to regain the energy lost. The second thing to remember is when you are feeling really good, don't over-do it. Try to regulate your energy to a good walk and a visit with friends. If you are feeling good try to find a healthy drink you enjoy and keep it handy as you just cannot drink too much.

I had fourteen sessions assigned for the first phase of chemo treatments. Each one is difficult to get through but my regiment became very routine for me. I would get the steroids and vitamins followed by the leucovorin, then a bag of oxaliplatin followed by my 5FU. The 5FU was attached to my port and put into a bag. It looked much like a man-purse which fed the chemo through my port over the next 46 hours while at home. Two days later I would return to the treatment center, have the tubes unhooked and go my merry way. I am not sure which is more deadly the cancer or the cure. I was able to go through thirteen sessions but knew that was all my body could take. It should have killed all of the microscopic cells by now anyway! The doctor agreed and I was officially off chemo therapy. I was now on the schedule for blood work to ensure the chemo did its job and to just check my CEA levels. This is a blood work make-up which indicates the amount of protein which is given off from your cancer cells. The normal range is 0-2.5 but if you begin to see an increase the cells are multiplying. My first reading was .3 and we hugged, high fived and was ready to lead the rest of my life as a Cancer survivor. I still needed to have blood work drawn every three months but it appeared like the cancer was gone. The longer you go without an increase, the better the probability the cancer was eradicated. My next scan was scheduled for March. We went to Florida for the winter and scheduled the blood draw at the Cleveland Clinic Weston facility. I could have had the blood draw anywhere but my experiences told me to stick with the Clinic. We made the two hour each way trip just to spend two minutes giving blood. The nurse would call me with my blood results. I was not worried as this was just the first draw of the many to come and was looking forward to joining the group of cancer survivors. Patti and I even bought a lot to build our retirement home in Fremont. It was on a golf course and was working with a contractor reviewing and revising our plans. I wanted everything on one floor with wide door frames in case we would ever need wheel chairs in our later years. This was interrupted by the results of the very first blood draw. My CEA increased to fifteen in three months. There was something somewhere but we just didn't know where. The job of discovery was left up to the PTSCANS. They are referred to as Pet Scans which are supposed to light up any cancer spots in your system. A very small spot was discovered in my lung but did not light up as cancer. They decided to wait a few months to schedule the surgery to see if there was any growth or additional nodules. It only took a few months to show up in the portal vein and on my liver once the surgery was completed to eradicate the tumor on the lung. The liver surgery was complete but the numbers did not decrease. They increased instead. It took several scans but it was determined it had spread again. It re-appeared on my lung and possibly a new growth near my pelvis. It was at this time the oncologist told me there was nothing more he could do as I was not responding to Chemotherapy. How could they know, as I have only been on the initial protocol chemo? Surgery has been their remedy from that point. We have not tried any other chemo and now he was telling me I was not responding. I had to have some answers and scheduled a meeting with the head of Oncology at the main Cleveland Clinic campus. This is when I became diligent in my chemotherapy research. Up to now I had totally relied on Dr. Fanning. I was now being totally proactive regarding my own chemotherapy. I researched chemotherapy for colon cancer and found many treatment options we have not tried. I listed them along with the side effects. Each has a specific job and even began to understand the purpose of each chemo. I was loaded for bear for my meeting with the head of Oncology. His first statement was I was not responding to the treatment and there was nothing more they can do. I asked him how they were certain as I never tried any treatments from my list. He was surprised as he was under the impression I had gone through the whole regiment of chemotherapy. He went down my list asking specifically about each one. I have never been on anything other than my first protocol treatment. He told me to set an appointment with Dr. Fanning as he would review with him some options going forward. He did tell me though my treatment may be limited as I had mutant K Ras and R Ras cells. I had no idea what that meant but I knew it probably was not good. Dr. Fanning explained how my cancer cells would probably not react from many of the chemotherapy options due to the mutant cells. Of course there was going to be an obstacle most people do not experience. It was in my Rhodes blood. The same DNA which caused my ancestors to fail repeatedly when they immigrated to the United States.

I reviewed with Dr. Fanning each chemo I had researched on my own. We haven't tried irinotecan with the 5 FU. We could use avastin with cetuximab. There was aflibercept, Yanitumumab, stivarga, ramucirumab or cyranza which targeted the vegf 2 receptor which helped the tumor get its nutrients. Each had its specific target and the use was in a specific order. I found through our conversation that physicians are also bound by the rules from the insurance companies. They could not recommend a particular chemotherapy without prior use of a different drug. It was a mixed-up crazy world of pharmaceutical companies, insurance and treatment. One thing I came to discover was each had its side effects. The most common are diarrhea, dehydration and nausea but there are hidden dangers such as rashes, high blood pressure or stroke. There are so many particulars that you need to be aware of its possibility and what to do if the side effect emerges. The side effects cause as many deaths as the cancer itself.

Chemotherapy was showing very little progress shrinking my cancer cells. I heard so much about the growing use of cannabis and the results. Physically I could tell I was deteriorating and was getting desperate to find alternative cures. There are so many options as an alternative to chemo around the world. Everyone had an opinion with a different brochure for each treatment. There were therapy alternatives in Thailand, Mexico and Europe among others. There were options to the options and it became mind boggling. The more I researched, I discovered the positive outcomes were not always based on good comparisons. There were outlandish claims of high recovery rates but upon further review I discovered the evaluations were based on stage one or stage two. I never felt comfortable leaving the United States for my treatment so decided to utilize what we had available in the country. Cannabis became my natural choice for an alternative treatment. Medicinal Cannabis is very different to street marijuana. I did not want to get high, I wanted to be cured. I was able to locate a registered licensed facility to purchase my treatment. I was impressed as they had a strict protocol and a detailed regiment of options for colon cancer. I tried it exclusively for six months but had poor results. My cancer grew in both numbers and size and my blood pressure became alarming high. My brief experiment with alternatives to chemotherapy was over. Although I am a skeptic regarding chemotherapy it is the only thing which slowed the growth for me. I could never understand how killing everything was going to abolish just the cancer. I thought it was like killing all the grass in your lawn to get to your weeds then hope only the grass grows back. Chemotherapy never made sense but it was all I had to fight the growth. Although my treatments were showing little progress, it was all I had. If I didn't fight with the chemo I would go quickly. It was not much of a choice but I wanted to find a treatment with little side effects which would not interrupt my desire to live out my life as normal as possible. We were able to find a new chemotherapy which has been proven effective, slowing the growth of the cancer cells. We decided on a half dose for half the recommended time to minimize the side effects. It was a great compromise for me.

9

FOLLOW-UP SURGERIES

My first surgery was at the time we discovered the tumor. It consisted of the initial tumor being removed from the colon, along with my ascending colon and half of the transcending colon. However due to going septic, I then had emergency surgery resulting in an open wound and an ostomy bag. My most anticipated surgery was eleven months later when I had surgery to reverse the ostomy. We heard so many stories where the ostomy could not be reversed so there were no guarantees I was going to be able to continue life without the bag. At this point I just finished my initial chemo of twenty two sessions. It was the standard treatment of leucavorin, 5FU and oxiplatin for colon cancer. I still had the bag but was off chemo and just waiting to get the reversal. This was the surgery I have been looking forward to for over nine months. We just got into our room at the Cleveland Clinic when we met a young woman walking the hallway post operation of her ostomy reversal. She was from New York and was told no one could perform the surgery to reverse her ostomy. She decided to try the Cleveland Clinic after being turned down by the famous New York medical establishment. The staff at the clinic assured her they could perform the surgery and she would be bag free. She was a young woman in her thirties and wanted to be ostomy free. The story gave me much hope going into this surgery. Of course I reminded Dr. Kessler hourly that I went septic on the last surgery and was expecting a smooth post-op this time around. He smiled and said he would take good care of me but nothing is a guarantee.

I went into surgery with two expectations; I wanted to wake up and wanted to be bag free. I was in the recovery room when I slowly came out of sedation. I opened my eyes looking at the familiar squares of the ceiling and thought to myself I was alive. The very next motion was to my side to check for the bag. There was no bag but a lot of bandages down the front on my stomach and the side where the stoma had been. They decided to close the open wound in my stomach area as it was almost healed anyway. It was truly a red letter day for the Rhodes family and I breathed a little prayer. Everything was out of my control anyway as it is totally in his hands. How many times have I heard to let it go as God was at the wheel? It is easier said than done. I thought to myself, put that on the list of things I need to work on.

My wishes were answered but I still had to pass gas and have a bowel movement. Now I realized why everyone walking the halls were wearing a t-shirt which read "I pooped today". It was the goal of everyone on the floor. You cannot check out of the hospital until your bowels are working. It took several days and a lot of walking but I finally accomplished my goal. I passed gas and had a bowel movement within hours of each other. I felt normal and was on the road to a cancer recovery. The doctor did explain my bowel habits would never be normal again but would not have to utilize an ostomy bag. He could not thoroughly explain what the changes would be, but I knew things were going to be different.

I went home to learn how to control my movements as I had chronic diarrhea. I went from not going for nine months to not holding my intake long enough to absorb the vitamins. It was a learning process with a definite change in diet. The learning process continued but with a small snag. The stomach started to produce grapefruit size hernias protruding from my stomach area.

Since the open wound was in my abdomen area, most of the muscles were cut out during my first surgery. There were just no stomach muscles left to keep the hernias from popping out. My reconstruction surgery was then scheduled for June. I was warned it would be a long painful recovery. Dr. Kessler recommended the only person to perform the surgery. Dr. Steven Rosenblatt is a specialist in gastrointestinal and laparoscopic hernia surgery. He was going to do the honors and had the type of personality that you would want to be his friend. He was upbeat, talkative but a world leader in abdominal surgery. I later learned he was well written in many articles in leading medical journals. We had a meeting to review exactly what he was going to do. He went into detail how he would need to cut and reposition most of my muscle from my back and side. I knew I was going to be sore for a while after this surgery. Dr. Kessler accompanied Dr. Rosenblatt during surgery in case there were any additional questions. It was a good thing they were both there as the surgery took much longer than anticipated as the scar tissue was everywhere. They spent as much time cutting away the scar tissue as they did fixing the hernias. The surgery was successful but they grossly underestimated the pain as most surgeons do. This was the most painful surgical recovery I have had to date. Every time I moved, the muscles in my body I would ache. He used and turned almost every muscle in my stomach, side and back. There was no comfortable position to relieve the pain. During the post operation appointment, Dr. Rosenblatt was amused at the number of scars on my abdomen from the various surgeries. He told me he was going to take a picture and send it to Beef Cake magazine. From that point on, I was affectionately called Beef Cake from he and his staff. I had the long scar from my chest to my abdominal area from the open wound. I also had the scar going sideways on my right side from the stoma removal. I now had another vertical scar along with several smaller areas from the tubes and drains. It really was not a pretty sight.

Three months into being cancer free, my March test CEA numbers indicated the cancer returned. The CEA number is the amount of protein the cancer cells put into the system. Although it is not an exact science it gives the growth tendencies of the cancer cells. The higher the number, the more the cells have metastasized. It is just a number to anyone else but to the patient it is everything. You have the blood drawn and wait for the call for the result of the CEA numbers. It was always several days after the blood draw but seemed like eternity. You are waiting for the number to see if the cancer spread. I was waiting for the call to see if the chemotherapy worked. The phone call came, the tumor marker was rising which only meant there was a growth of cancer cells somewhere in the body. The numbers were going up so they had to find the area of concern. Obviously, for me, the initial tumor was in the colon but the oncologist knew early on it already metastasized. The CTSCAN was the next scenario. They found the culprit. It was a small nodule on the lung. We were scheduled a review with the lung specialist and decided to schedule surgery for August. I already had the surgery scheduled for June with Dr. Rosenblatt, two months earlier. Could my body handle two major surgeries back to back?

The problem I was now facing was the nodule which was discovered on my lung had to be eradicated. I was still recovering from the reconstruction in June with the lung surgery in August. This would be my sixth major surgery in less than two years. I was concerned whether my body could handle another beating from surgery. Dr. Sudith Murthy was recommended to perform my surgery. I did a little research and found he was the Section Head of Thoracic Surgery. His credentials were endless as he graduated head of his class at Columbia. He was a resident and intern at Harvard receiving many scholar awards. I was very fortunate to have Dr. Murthy willing to perform my surgery. We had several meetings and he assured me after what Dr. Rosenblatt did to me this would be a walk in the park. The tumor never "lit up" through all the PTSCANS as cancer is designed to do so I mentioned to Dr. Murthy the nodule probably was not cancer as he thought. He jokingly told me if it walks like a duck, quacks like a duck it is a duck. He was right, this surgery was much easier than my last one with Dr. Rosenblatt but the recovery was a lot more interesting. I woke with a garden hose sticking out of my back and it was difficult to turn as I was still sore from my escapades with Dr. Rosenblatt six weeks earlier. We were waiting for Dr. Murthy to visit that next morning and heard the loud shoes on the tile floor coming our way. The person who burst through the door had a big, familiar smile. It was my son David who drove to be there when I awoke from the surgery. It was such a pleasant surprise. All of a sudden the pain of the surgery went away for that brief moment. During our hugs and kisses with David we did not notice that Dr. Murthy entered the room. The first thing Dr. Murthy said to me was, "it was cancer, like I said, but I got it all". I think he was secretly saying I know more than the scans. Dr. Murthy was a well-renowned surgeon but was less jovial than his counterparts. He was a very matter of fact type person, which was fine with me as long as he was a good surgeon! The surgery was scheduled for a couple hours, but true to form, took about six hours. He reviewed the surgery ever so briefly but looked square into my eyes and said he would never do surgery on me again. It took him so much longer because of the mass amount of scar tissues I had everywhere in my body. He echoed what everyone of his predecessor have told us. Every previous surgery took longer than expected due to the amount of scar tissue they would encounter. The volume of scar tissue was produced either by surgeries or the result of the large amount of poisons when I went septic. This made surgery very difficult and timely.

I was recovering well but I still had a few drains in me. I knew I had to walk to avoid pneumonia settling in the lungs. Those large drains made it hard. I pushed myself but was difficult to walk the hospital halls as it was painful just to turn or get out of bed. It was tough to maneuver with the tubes and the garden hose size drain sticking out of my back. Dr. Murthy was right, though, whatever he did was much easier than what my friend Dr. Rosenblatt put me through. I knew walking was the key to recovery and pushed myself relentlessly. The nurses were encouraging but also very impressed by my tenacity. They asked me to talk to some of the other patients who were hesitant to walk on their own. It was difficult to have a conversation at first as they were recovering and didn't want another patient bothering them. As the conversation would move forward they became more comfortable. The talks would always center on their surgeries, which opened the door for me to tell them my story. Once I showed them my scars from the other recent surgeries and shared the importance the walks were on my road to recovery, they decided they would make the effort to walk after all. My scars were still bright red as they were not totally healed. The other patients could see what I had recently been through and was still pushing myself to walk. I think it may have given them the courage they needed to get out of bed. I understood my scars tell a story and were no longer an area to hide. I began to realize my story is unique and could resonate with people going through a similar crisis. Most of all, I was still smiling and had a positive attitude. Concentrating on the blessings were putting me in the frame of mind needed to overcome this terrible disease.

We eliminated the tumor in the lung which had to be the source of the high tumor marker numbers. The latest test showed the numbers have not decreased at all. The oncologist suggested we just wait to see if they are just slow in decreasing. We waited until January, five months later. The numbers were slowly increasing which indicated more cancer. It was time for another CTSCAN. The radiologist discovered a new tumor on the portal vein. The decision was ultimately made not to perform surgery as it was quite risky. It was located in an area where it was hard to reach and they thought my body could not handle another major surgery that soon. We stayed on the schedule to monitor the blood work and numbers. We continued this agenda until the next scan. They found a new, larger tumor on the liver. This one was operable and needed to be eradicated. It would be too dangerous to leave it on my liver. The tumor was found in February and was referred to Dr. Eren Berber. He was the associate professor of surgery at the Cleveland Clinic and the director of Robotic Endocrine Surgery and co-director of Liver Tumor Ablation Program. If I had to have another surgery he was definitely the man I would prefer. He decided on a late March surgery date. That made for seven surgeries in less than 2 ½ years and I was a little nervous going into another major surgery on March 29th. However, once they discovered the cancer on the liver I was very anxious to have it removed. I lost too many friends when the cancer metastasized to the liver. This one scared me and I wanted the tumor out. I had such a great sense of urgency. I pushed for an earlier surgery date and even asked them to call me if there were any cancellations. We were wintering in Florida and told them I could be there in several days if necessary. They did have a cancellation and called me on a Monday for a Friday surgery. I declined as my mind became accustomed to the March 29th date. I was like an athlete which needed time to mentally prepare for the upcoming game. I felt we would have been too hurried and would not be going into the surgery with a relaxed, more confident state of mind.

The pre-op routine was scheduled which consist of blood work, x-rays, EKG, stress test and counseling with the anesthesiologist and surgeon. The last doctor we saw was Dr. Berber at the end of the day. He told us we were a "go" for the surgery and he also explained a new technique called ICG dye fluorescent Image with pinpoint camera. It consisted of a dye being injected into my body the day before the surgery. The body would dissipate the dye with the exception of where the cancer was on the liver. During surgery they would be able to recognize where the cancer was located for easier identification and removal. Once they were able to locate the cancer spots they were easily removed. Dr. Berber was anticipating taking up to forty percent of my liver so any advantage we could have I was willing to try. During surgery the decision proved to be successful. Rather than taking forty percent of the liver they only needed to take out five percent. This new technique saved most of my liver but also gave him additional time in surgery. There was a new problem. The cancer was throughout the Vena cava Vein which was hidden from the scans as it was on the back side of the vein. This was not anticipated going into the surgery. This was a very delicate extraction and required the Cleveland Clinic transplant team to remove and repair this section. I was later told there was not a handful of hospitals in the country who could have provided this service with the amount of expertise needed to perform this function of the surgery. Dr. Berber then took it upon himself to go after the cancer on the portal vein. He needed to take out the gall bladder and cut out more scar tissue to get to the well-hidden tumor. He later told me he was not the type of surgeon to leave any cancer behind. The surgery lasted over nine hours but was a complete success. If I had scheduled surgery sooner we would not have been aware of the new dye technique leaving no time to continue the surgery. It was strange how everything appeared to happen for a reason. Either way, I was glad to open my eyes in the recovery room and know I was alive.

Due to the seriousness and length of the surgery only two visitors could be allowed in post op at a time. Patti and Sarah came in first and I was so delighted to see them. My sister, Cheryl, and brother, Mike, were next and I had this overwhelming need to tell them that I was now aware it was our mom who has been watching over me. I don't know why it was important to tell them. I had this new found knowledge that my mom has been the one looking over me through my life. I cannot recall having a vision as your conscious does not remember anything during the surgery. Knowing my mother, who died when I was six, was watching over me gave me such peace. I know this is the same feeling of peace a Christian feels knowing they are being watched by Jesus Christ.

Several days after surgery my throat would hurt when I tried to shave. I asked the surgeon what could be the cause of this irritation. He was a little hesitant to tell me but during the surgery they actually lost me on the table. They had to revive me through the curated artery. I actually died on the table and they brought me back to life. It was no longer a coincidence to me that I had this new found information regarding my mother being my guardian angel. I reflected on the many times I avoided an accident at the very last moment. The many times my conscious "talked" me out of doing the wrong thing. It was always my mother who I could barely remember. This instantly made me want to be a better person and I thought of my many decisions in the past which must have greatly disappointed her. I could not change the past but going forward I would be a better person. No more grudges, ungrateful rhetoric or malice towards other people. I had a change of heart almost instantly. I always had a smile on my face but not always in my heart. Things were going to be different in my heart going forward.

It took several days for us to hear all the information from the surgery. We were getting bits and pieces but were adding up to one phenomenal performance by the surgeons of the Cleveland Clinic. I was given a great compliment during recovery as several of the surgeons from my previous surgeries stopped by my room to chat. They heard of the surgery around the Clinic campus and wanted to say hello and talk about the surgery. My understanding was it was the talk of the OR area. Dr. Berber was showing the pictures of the repair work and the tumor on the portal vein. He showed Patti so she had to take a photo of the picture on his phone. It was rather intriguing but also a little scary that so much was going on inside my body without me knowing it. Dr. Rosenblatt, who always called me "Beefcake," came to the room and told me his nurse was in the OR area and heard about my case. She went back to his office telling him some patient who had colon cancer was in liver surgery, and they had to call in the by-pass team. He asked was it Mr. Rhodes by any chance? She was surprised he knew who the patient was by name. I was the talk of the medical campus. My surgeries were becoming legendary around the Cleveland Clinic, at least in my mind. My surgeons possess a world renowned skill and I was very fortunate to be their patient. They became good friends as each were not only great surgeons but wonderful people.

My friends and family have always been a large support but at this particular surgery, Joe Greco, friend from Canada, who we met at our condo complex came to the hospital to be with us for several days. We became close friends as both of his sisters lived in our complex. He would visit around the pool as our community is very active and a lot of fun. We began talking and became close friends as we had so much in common. We joked about not being normal as our sense of humor is off the wall but we totally understood each other. Joe was one of the nicest people you would ever meet. He stood about 6'4" and was well over 300 pounds and reminded me of Tony Soprano from the Sopranos. His heart is as big as his stature and everyone loves the man. What drew me to him was his love of his family and his work ethic which included high principles. This was how I conducted my business life and respected others who handled themselves in the same fashion. He insisted on staying at the hotel which was attached to the hospital. He would tear up every time he told others how Patti stayed with me for months in the hospital sleeping on folding chairs or in the window sills. He said he would come each morning so Patti could be relieved to take a normal shower and catch some sleep if she could, at the hotel. He promised to not leave my side while she was gone. This was the only way he could convince her to take some time away. Each morning for four days he would come into the room at 7:30 with coffee and a pastry for the two of them and allow Patti to feel normal for a couple hours. He would sit for hours on an uncomfortable hospital chair just to be a friend. Again, the many blessings were manifesting itself through the tribulations of the cancer. Joe and I had a great friendship but would have never known the depth of our relationship if not for the surgery. I would prefer not to have cancer but I was beginning to embrace the blessings I was receiving rather than dwelling on all the negatives.

10

STRENGTH FROM OTHERS

My family is my hero. My wife, Patti in particular. She was not going to leave my side and was my rock through it all. Her being next to me saved my life on more than one occasion and no doubt saved my sanity. After I came out of ICU after my second surgery, I tried not to go to sleep. I had to have the lights on as I knew I would die if I went to sleep. She was patient and would be there for me only leaving to shower, eat and change clothes. I cannot stress to the caregivers and family members enough to offer strength to the patient as they first need a strong will to live. It is very easy to become negative and depressed but you have to put an emphasis on looking at the blessings instead of the negatives of cancer. We have always had a strong family bond but as the kids got older, developed their own family and moved away, we realized we are not the epicenter of their world. That is the natural progression of life. The transition of the family was hard for me but I soon discovered their love for me did not change. I was confusing being a guiding parent and love. I needed their love and support now. That love was as needed as much as the medicine to get me through some very dark, depressing times. You need the will to fight and survive. You need to target that driving force to keep you going. For me, the target and will to survive was simple: family. My desire and will was no longer to be their parent, but to continue to be their friend.

As I mentioned previously, our friends called us the Brady Bunch as we did almost everything as a family. If one of us had to go to the mall, we all went and made a day of it. We were a very close group and stayed close until the job and spouses called them to a different direction. I was struggling with this internally when I was diagnosed as one son was in Boston and the other in Phoenix while I was in Fremont, Ohio. I was told sons are usually different than daughters as they take the wife's family as their own. It was hard to not be needed on a daily basis. My daughter and her family stayed in our hometown and remained close, so there was that bond that cemented our ties. My youngest son stayed in town but was not married and still sowing oats. I was reminded how much my life meant to my daughter, Sarah, when I was recovering in my hospital room. She was sitting next to my bed in the hospital rubbing my arm. The nurse made me move to another spot in the room and she moved her chair to be next to me continuing rubbing my arm. She was just talking to me but rubbing my arm the whole time. She never let go. The old saying "a son is a son until he takes a wife, but a daughter is a daughter her entire life" can be very true. This observation reminded me that Sarah would always be my little girl.

The fact that two of my sons lived out of town but made it to the hospital on a regular basis was a true testament to our relationship. Life goes on; however, and the family settles into their routine as you continue to fight the daily struggles. This is when the strength from others is needed the most. The support to get through those daily fights is so important and requires a lot of energy which you really don't have. It is from your family, friends and community that you gain the strength and vigor to fight. I was so grateful to at least have two of the kids, Sarah and Tim, close to home. I gained so much strength from being around family but especially the grandchildren. They were so thoughtful and considerate. Tim's daughter, Havana would come in and say "how is your stomach today Papack?" She associated my cancer to the many surgeries and I knew she must have been warned to be careful around my stomach. Zoe is Sarah's only daughter and is a grandfather's delight. She has her mom's mannerisms and deep concerns. She was afraid to sit on my lap as she didn't want to hurt my stomach but would speak to me with a low deliberate tone asking if I felt good that day. Havana and Zoe are best friends as they are about the same age. If they have not seen each other for two weeks they would let out a shriek of joy when they finally got together. It was delightful to watch them and they always brought a smile to my face. The family was my strength which I needed on a regular basis. It made me feel normal even though there were the ever present pains of cancer which always brought me to reality. Sometimes I would call for a family cookout even though I was tired and drained. I needed that vitality of the hustle only a family cookout can bring. I tried to live my motto that cancer would not take a day away from me, but there were some very difficult days to pull it all together with a smile on my face. I think Sarah could always see through me as she would collect the family and say it was time to go home. Although sad to see the day end so early, I was also grateful to have my rest time. It was always the cancer telling my body to repose.

My friends are so special to me. They were always such a big part of my therapy and strength to remain positive. My good friend, Joe Greco, already made several trips to Fremont from Toronto. He was at my door two days after getting out of rehabilitation. He made a trip in the depth of winter just to spend a couple days with us. This was the first time he was able to see me in person since I was first admitted into the hospital. He wanted to drive us to our doctor appointments and be with us when I had the port installed. He knew Patti didn't like to drive, let alone in the middle of a snow storm. It was now June and he wanted to make another visit. He brought his sisters who were also our good friends from our condo association. We were both excited for their visit. We made plans to show them the area and took them on the drive around the lake which I came to love so much. Joe and Sue Albrechta, our good friends in Fremont, hosted a dinner at their home. Joe purchased a beautiful estate when it was on the verge of demolition. They spent years bringing the home to its turn of the century beauty. It is a large home with an elegant dining room with hand painted murals. They offered to host a dinner for Joe and his sisters along with a few other friends in the area. They displayed their stylish tableware which they found in the attic of their historic home. It was a very chic affair and I appreciated the generosity they extended to our Canadian friends. One point after the meal, everyone was getting a tour of the home while Joe and I spent some time to ourselves sitting at the dining room table. Joe and have had many deep, personal conversations and quickly got lost in another one sitting at the table. Suddenly, without warning, he leaned to one side and passed gas. It was loud and all he could do was chuckle as he was too embarrassed to explain himself. The smell permeated the room with an odor as pungent as it was loud. At that moment everyone busted through the old butler doors into the dining room and we could tell the odor stopped them in their tracks. He quickly looked at me and said, "You left a good one that time." He was proud of himself as he thought he avoided a lot of embarrassment and had no problem throwing me under the bus to save face. I started laughing and said, Not this time buddy! I have an ostomy bag and could not pass gas if I wanted to. He was exposed and everyone laughed until we could not laugh any more. That was the much needed icebreaker with the group. Everyone took turns that night telling their most embarrassing moments and the laughter flowed until late into the evening. Joe would retell the story many times to our friends in Florida. The week he and his sisters spent with us in Fremont was a much needed relief from our daily routine. That night of laughter put us back into the world of living. I was able to make light of my ostomy bag with the help of my friend. The gorilla now left the room and I noticed our friends were much more comfortable asking us tough questions.

It is so important to have the support of your friends and family and to keep them updated with your treatments and prognosis. It is important to realize everyone in your support group will handle your cancer differently. However, I always kept my family informed so they could feel a part of the process. Sarah was very involved with us, helping Patti whenever she could. Nate and Dave were far away from my daily struggles and I know they had their own lives to live but we would update them whenever we would talk. Tim lived in the area and would see me often when he was not working. Nate's way of coping was to call me almost every day just to say hello which meant the world to me. Dave's method was the opposite as he began to pull back from the family. I reminded myself it was his way of coping with the cancer. I understand this is common among family members, especially if they are particularly close. Although very common, this method of coping was harder for me to accept as I would have given everything I own to have a conversation with my father. My dad passed away three years before I was diagnosed and I was glad he did not have to see me in this fight as it would have hurt him terribly. My dad was the reason I moved back to Ohio from California. He worked himself into a mental breakdown on his decision to retire. He was an independent insurance agent and did not want to work hard enough to keep the office open but had no hobbies to keep his mind occupied in retirement. I was living the corporate life in Los Angeles and was just offered the position of Vice President of Sales for the west coast with an upcoming company called RPS, the forerunner of FedEx Ground. It was an offspring of Roadway Express where I was the Sales Manager in the Los Angeles area. It was a very difficult decision as I was a thirty four year old father of four with an offer of a lifetime. On the other hand I had a father in need who gave up everything to raise his family. My father grew up an orphan and would occasionally tell us the stories of the Marsh Foundation in Van Wert, Ohio, where he was raised. My mother died when we were all young and dad continued to be both mother and father to his four children. He was a metro man before the term was ever coined. He worked all day, cooked at night and did the laundry in the spare time. I loved and respected him as he gave me so much guidance in my life. He was a man who grew up with no family and taught each of us that having a family is a precious gift. As I look back it really wasn't a difficult decision. He never knew the real reason we moved back to Fremont as I made up some story that it was a great place to raise a family. He didn't need to know I made the move to work with him in his office so he didn't have to worry about the cost. He no longer had the pressure to work hard enough to maintain the office, I was there. If I ever had any doubts about my decision they were erased at his funeral. I loved the time we had together and the time he had with my children. Nothing would have been the same if I would have accepted the position instead of making the move to Fremont. Time is one thing you can never have back. He instilled the importance of family in me, which was the reason my family was so crucial in my fight with cancer. I had to have a motive to fight this ongoing battle. They were my reason, they gave me that motivation to live by their constant encouragement.

Patti was always more than just a part of my support team. She was there for every appointment and every chemo treatment. We found two sets of ears are almost imperative during your appointments. As a patient, I heard less than half what the doctor was telling us. Patti and I would disagree what we remembered until we read her notes. Sometimes we were both wrong about what we thought he was saying to us. Sarah was our initial note taker at the hospital while going through my first set of surgeries. Patti picked up the responsibility when we started our follow-up appointments. She became very proficient recording the drain output, my daily blood pressure and the wound details while I was in the rehabilitation center. It made the nurse's job much easier as they were hesitant to even accept a patient like me at their facility. The appointments became a natural act for her, always carrying her well-worn brown leather notepad. It is important to have a partner with you for even the most minor doctor appointments. By contrast, I had a very good friend who was diagnosed with intestinal cancer and had issues remembering anything the doctor would tell him. He was very scared when he was diagnosed with cancer and could not recall anything else the doctor said at their initial appointment. I was in Florida for the winter but flew home to visit him and discuss what was ahead. We were instantly best friends from the time I was introduced to him at age twelve. His real name was John but he was known as Squirrel to anyone who knew him. The nickname came from my cousin who was chasing him around the neighborhood until John finally climbed a tree and stayed there until my cousin gave up, saying he was nothing more than a squirrel. The nickname stuck through his adult life. He was the kind of guy where innocent trouble would follow him everywhere, which instantly drew me to him. His personality was infectious as he became a friend to anyone he would meet. Our school years mirrored the sitcom The Wonder Years, with him and me maturing during an age of innocence. We were never far away from each other and every weekend was filled with new adventures.

Squirrel was very nervous and anxious about the treatment, prognosis and lifestyle changes he would encounter. It was difficult for me to offer positive encouragement as I could see how his body was quickly deteriorating. I was fighting my own issues to stay positive. However, I found the more reassurance I would give him the more positive I felt about my own prospects. Helping my close friend gave me strength and confidence to address my own cancer. His was a non-curable form of cancer but I always tried to instill in him the need to stay positive. The mind can perform wonderful things and assured him the cure was just around the corner. His family was very supportive even though his brothers and sisters lived all over the country. Someone went with him to every appointment. Our mutual friend, Steve Frost, would take John to his appointments and take the much needed notes. I was impressed as everyone took turns coming home to visit and get him out of the house. John had a mentally challenged son which took most of his wife's energy. She had trouble balancing her time between their son and the energy to be an effective caregiver. The family responded as the substitute caregiver. It was very difficult for me to watch my friend deteriorate throughout the next year. I could tell the end was imminent but we would still discuss the need to stay positive until that call would come from the doctors saying they discovered the cure. His final winter, we came from Florida several times to see my friend only to find him continually declining. My final visit was on a Sunday in February where we talked and laughed about the many escapades of our youth. He was there the first time I built up the courage to kiss a girl. He was there when I was married and was by my side when I got a divorce. Now I was watching my good friend getting ready to make his next journey. We took our pictures, kissed goodbye and I flew off to Florida only to get a phone call four days later that he has passed. It was a very tough time for me as we were so very close and I have watched so many go the way of my friend John. There was a lot of soul searching on my trip back to Florida after the funeral. So many are affected and there is still so little progress regarding a cure. I wanted John to be cured so badly. I loved my friend and knew he trusted me. I wanted to be right and tell him I told you so, I knew you would make it. I miss my friend John.

I went back to Florida to my second family of support, my winter family. I was nervous about taking that first trip, and upgraded to first class to avoid contact with as many people as possible. During the flight, I noticed the adhesive section of my ostomy bag was pulling away from my skin and it was about ready to break. I silently whispered to Patti about my situation and asked her to meet me in the restroom at the front of the plane to help me change the bag. We barely fit into the restroom. We had to position ourselves very carefully for her to work on my ostomy. I pulled my shirt up high enough for her to gain access to the stoma, all the while we were clumsily banging into the sides of the small bathroom walls.

We finally finished and exited the bathroom looking directly into the smiling faces of the other passengers. I embarrassedly sat in my seat, as I knew they saw my ostomy bag and the repair kit. Slowly, I started to realize why they were all smiling. I began to understand that they were not laughing at my handicap, they thought I had just become a member of the "mile-high club".

We were so fortunate to have a great group of friends at our condo association in Florida. It was a community of friendly, caring people. It is an older community but the people make the area alive with sun worshipper's gossip, the recipe sharing conversations and of course, the ever present discussions on which restaurants have the best bargains. The sun made me flourish compared to the cold in Ohio. Everyone was so active it was a little easier to forget my woes and I continued to be in the world of the living. That first winter it was still difficult to sit poolside though, as I still had the open wound and ostomy bag. I wanted to keep my midsection covered and hidden from our friends. We purchased a few tank tops so I could continue to socialize with everyone. I was still a little hesitant to be at the pool and was sure my friends sensed my embarrassment. My mind was put to ease when Mary Greco, Joe's sister, bought me a tank top which she thought would be big enough to hide the bag. It gave me the understanding they all knew about my bag and that I had nothing to hide. It was a considerate sign of empathy with an intended message; to let it go and be part of the community.

My chemo continued while in Florida including having to wear the chemo bag for two days during treatment week. I did not want to go out in public during those two days. We would do our errands and go to the homes of close friends but never to a high traffic restaurant. My friend, Joe Greco, loved to go to the Blue Martini, an upscale nightclub in Naples every Tuesday night. He convinced me to try it for one night. Our friends, Robert and Wendy, are an outstanding musical group and were contracted to play the Blue every Tuesday evening. We had a large group anchored by our other friends, Tony and Fran Ferrari. They are New York transplants with that heavy New York accent but with open hearts which would make a stranger melt. Joe had his same table every Tuesday so we knew it would be easy for Patti and me to go and sit for a while. We didn't have to wait for a table and Joe assured me he would save me a seat. That first night of trial there was a large group of us and we were able to mingle around the table with everyone. One man in particular, who I had never met, kept talking to me and following me around the table. He was telling me all about himself and his wealth, I thought he was trying to impress me. I found the man to be very self-absorbent and decided to excuse myself to the bathroom. When I was out of earshot he asked Patti if I had been seeing Joe very long as he thought I was cute. He told her his big attraction to me was my handsome man purse. He thought I was with Joe and my chemo bag was a man purse. Hearing the story, I realized I was assimilating just fine and no longer had any reservations wearing my chemo bag. I began to enjoy life each day. We lived like any other couple who retired in Florida except I could not go swimming and had chemo treatment every other week. Our condo decor changed a little as Patti continued to change my wound and ostomy bag on a daily basis. We moved a table into the bedroom so she had a large table to work from. She was so particular it was almost like a hospital room. It was a little crowded but at least we were out of the cold in Ohio. It seemed when I needed family the most, someone would take the time to fly to Florida to spend time with us. My son, Nate, was the first to make the visit. It was unannounced and very welcomed. He lives in Arizona so I was confident it was not the sun which drew him to make this surprise detour from his busy schedule as a Southwest Pilot. In order to spend time with us, he had to fly his weekly schedule, then get a flight to Florida. He then had to go directly back to work for his next week's schedule, all without seeing his family. We knew he was making a very big sacrifice to be with us and was greatly appreciated. It was just what I needed to lift my spirits during those long days of recovery. Although we were in Florida less than six weeks that first winter, Nate, my brother Mike and sister, Cheryl each took time to visit us. Even Sarah was able to make a schedule change to make a long weekend visit with us. It was such a wonderful break from that first winter of surgeries, hospitals and therapy.

Every winter in Florida thereafter I missed the kids and grandchildren but Sarah would make it a point to visit at least twice a winter. I wasn't sure if it was to see me or get out of the cold, either way we both benefitted from her visits. Sarah's family is so easy going and it was always a pleasure to have her visit. Patti and I would look forward to our time together with her in Florida. Carter, Sarah's son, even nicknamed our condo "The Friendship House". We tried to make it a week of fun and relaxation for everyone. For Carter it was a week watching the wildlife at the beach and chasing the frogs and geckos around our complex. They could pick anywhere to go on vacation but they loved the beach and the pool as much as we did! I am one of those people who like to beat the crowds and Sarah always capitulated with my request to leave for the beach by 8:00 A.M. I wanted to get a good parking space before the parking lot sharks would start circling to find their own space to park. It was easier to get up a little earlier than to circle the area looking for a parking space. Sarah was very conscious of our idiosyncrasies especially when it came to keeping the condo spotless. She would accommodate us by keeping everything clean and put away. It was her way of saying she was a great guest and wants to come back. It was the therapy I needed, I need to be around family.

The following Thanksgiving we spent in Florida with Sarah and the family. Our plans were to come home for the holidays and head back to Florida the day after Christmas. Cancer can change the best plans. This time I received a call from one of my closest female friends. Mary Kaye married my friend's brother when we were in high school. We all got along and became very close when I married her niece four years later. She and Vince were one of the best things which developed from my marriage. I became Godfather to their first born, Jamie, and we remain close to this day. The day we got home from Florida, which was the Monday following Thanksgiving, I received a call from Mary Kaye. She wanted to talk as she went to the doctor the Wednesday before Thanksgiving for a sonogram to find the cause of her acid reflux. She was very surprised when she received the diagnosis on Monday that, in fact, she had advanced pancreatic cancer. It had already spread to the liver to the point there were signs of the liver already shutting down. We all had lunch on Tuesday and she was telling us her symptoms and diagnosis. She knew there was no hope and referred to herself as a walking dead woman. We gingerly joked about our situation but spoke about the need to stay positive. She said she just needed to get everything in order as her concern was not with herself but Vince and her family. Vince was a retired heavy equipment operator and an avid golfer but never wrote a check in his life. She kept all the records, wrote all the checks and managed the investments. She needed help with the transition. Mary Kaye was one of the loveliest people I knew but also possessed a no nonsense type of personality. She knew her situation and time was of the essence. I would help any way possible but was sure she had more time than she expected. We saw her one week later and she was already half way through her final agenda. Her skin tone and color was already changing and it finally hit me that she was probably correct in her own health assessment. She was fighting time to get her list completed. I realized how fortunate I was in my fight as I had time to digest my situation and maintain hope. Mary Kaye's sunshine was her grandchildren. She did not want them to see her quick decline and kept a strong presence during the times they saw her over the next month. She told me she was able to handle anything on her journey except when she told her grandson her condition. It was the hardest thing she had ever done. She insisted he hear it straight from her. She didn't realize how hard that conversation would be for her. It was hard for me to tell my own children let alone discuss with my adult grandchildren. I can only imagine how hard it was for her to discuss with Wyatt, her oldest grandchild, about her pending demise. She saw the doctor the day before Thanksgiving and died Christmas morning. She waited until the family was there to let herself go. It was appropriate as Christmas was Mary Kaye's favorite day of the year. She gave me strength to be brave if the prognosis isn't a cure.

Mary Kaye did not have a chance to be a cancer survivor. She could not fight that struggle where everyone offers encouragement to be strong and beat cancer. Not everyone wins. This was sinking in to me. I was allowing the negatives to enter my thought pattern. Mary Kaye fought one of the bravest battles with dignity but did not have the chance to stay positive. She barely had time to get her list completed. I have that chance and was going to go forward. I pushed the negatives aside and started counting the positives again. It may not turn out the way I hope but am going to face the future with dignity.

Positive help comes in many strange ways. Just letting the person know you are thinking about them is important. I had so many friends send me cards on a regular basis. Cards of encouragement, cards of prayers, notes to let me know I was in their prayer group, it was so uplifting. I received so many from people I barely knew but they wanted to let me know I was in their thoughts. I can never tell all those people how much this meant to me. If I would see them on the street I would let them know how special their note was to me. I could see the smile of appreciation on their face. Most people do not send cards for recognition but do appreciate it when they are noted. It is just human nature to be appreciated. Just a phone call or note to let them know you are thinking about them is probably one of the most positive motivators you can do for a person. On the contrary, when a friend or family member does not call or contact you it creates a heavy heart. I spoke to many patients and all of them felt the need to have close contact with friends and family throughout their treatment. Some people are afraid to make the call because they don't know what to say, so they don't call at all. Be normal and don't be afraid to ask the questions you want to ask. Try not to blurt out the names of all the people you know who died from cancer though. Keep in mind the patient's needs to stay positive. I have met with many cancer patients who struggle to stay positive. The ones with the most issues were the ones who received little contact or support from their family. I witnessed church members who gave up their own personal time to help a fellow congregation member get to chemo treatments, clean their homes or help with daily chores. You don't know how much this meant to them as it is one less thing needing to be done. It may be a little thing but when you are so tired it is hard to eat, any little completed chore is a big blessing.

On our first trip home from Florida, our friends at the Fremont Yacht Club surprised us with a welcome home party. Joe and Sue picked us up at the Cleveland airport and asked if we would like to go to the yacht club. My first reaction was I was too tired. Joe had to spoil the surprise and tell me the group got together to have a party in our honor for our trip back to Fremont. We were only gone six weeks but this gave them an opportunity to show us how much they loved us both. They had a big sign made reading "Welcome home Jack," and had over thirty people waiting to greet us. This meant so much to Patti and me. What a special thing to do for us. It was so easy to feel blessed at that moment.

The physical struggles as well as the mental can keep you negative. People would ask me what it was like to be on chemo and my only comparison was having the flu with a hangover on steroids. Of course some treatments are harsher than others as I have seen people fly through chemo like they are having tea with a friend. Every cancer is different, every patient is different and every patient using the same chemo is different. There are no rules, only a few guidelines of historical reactions called side-affects. There were some chemotherapy where I had no reactions while others were severely understated. Every patient reacts differently to chemo but one thing every patient has in common is the need for support. Chemotherapy can get you down both physically and mentally as you have a tendency to be tired. Having friends who know these struggles can help overcome those depressing days. I was blessed in so many ways. Friends who understand that a night out does not mean a whole night out. There are times when you want to go out and feel normal but can only last so long. It is great to have those friends who understand and will end the night early without making you feel like you ruined their night out. Our close friends, Joe and Sue Albrechta, have always been there for us. They are the type of friends who empty the trash at your son's graduation party just because they see you need help. They always say and do the right thing. We were so blessed to have them as close friends. He is our family attorney as well as my best friend. He and Sue drove to the clinic in Cleveland the night before my first surgery to review my trust, power of attorney and other papers to be sure it was completed exactly how we wanted. It has been some time since they were reviewed and he knew I would be thinking of those financial things. He didn't want me worried about little things going into surgery. They would make the two hour drive at least three times a week to be sure Patti had what she needed as well as supply her with a little sweet snacks to keep her going. Anyone who knows Patti knows about her sweet tooth. They would always greet us with a big smile and somehow knew exactly how long to stay.

Your friends and family mean so much in a normal life but is exaggerated even more so when fighting the fight of cancer. As a patient, you have to look at the good in everything on a daily basis. It is too easy to fall into the "poor me" syndrome. Look around at your friends all asking what they can do. My brother, Mike, and sister, Cheryl, lived in Arizona so could not visit as often as they would like but a day did not go by when they would not let me know they were thinking of me. My sister is very spiritual and would send a daily thought or prayer each morning. She was so positive and could find the good with most anything or anyone. She was always my cheerleader able to find the good in the daily struggle. Mike is the more direct sibling. He would always do the research and find the optimistic outcomes and positive percentages with my surgeries and the cancer itself. I preferred not to research the averages of recovery, just the chemo itself and their intentions in its fight against the cancer cell. Both siblings remain supportive on a daily basis. The old saying you can't pick your family may be true, but in my case, I was truly blessed with my siblings. My mom passed away when we were all young and we were raised by a remarkable man but we always leaned on each other for that daily support. We are fortunate as we have kept that very close bond through our lives. We have always been close but their individual strengths have been a big factor in my recovery.

Ask your friends and family for help. Let them in to your daily needs, don't shut them out. You will find they are all too willing to help with all your needs. We have neighbors who have their lawn cut by friends who want to help but don't know what else to do. It turns out they love to do lawn work and are very happy to do it for a friend in need. Ask them what they would like to do as you will need help in a lot of areas. You can even give them a list of your needs and allow them to pick one which best suits their schedules. Open your heart and allow your friends and family into your life with cancer. You will find blessing in so many ways you never thought possible. Cancer is a terrible illness but embrace the many good things and changes you have encountered by being diagnosed. You will be amazed how your friends become even closer and acquaintances become close friends.

PICTURES

Above Left: The sign says, "You became a survivor on the day you were diagnosed." A great motto for all cancer patients taken at MD Anderson in Houston, Texas. Above Right: My Cleveland Clinic treatment center nurses Felicia and Lynn.

The Fremont Yacht Club surprised me with a welcome home party.

Above Left: My brother Mike, also a cancer survivor, toasting to our many blessings. Above Right: Joe Greco, Patti and me at the Blue Martini. Notice my chemo bag which was mistaken for a man purse.

Below Left: Our close friends Joe and Sue Albrechta
Below Right: Patti and I living life daily.

My loving children David, Tim, me, Sarah and Nate

On the beach after my first two surgeries. Notice the ostomy bag from under my tank top.

Above Left: My son Tim and me enjoying a Cleveland Indians game between chemo treatments. Above Right: My son David on a surprise visit to the Cleveland Clinic.

Nathan surprised me with four quarts of fresh Florida orange juice flown in from Sun Harvest in Fort Myers.

Nate on a visit to Florida the first winter after my initial set of surgeries.

My last visit with my good friend John "Squirrel" Werling.
My best friend since twelve years old.

11

STAY POSITIVE

The one thing I proclaimed from the very beginning was: Cancer may take my life but it was not going to take a day of living away from me. I wanted to enjoy my life as long as I could physically do so. My son, David, gave me a book for Christmas on the power of living positive. It should be mandatory reading for all cancer patients. The book is Love, Medicine & Miracles by Dr. Bernie Siegel. It was the support and reinforcement I needed to stay positive in my own belief system. I knew miracles could happen, but only to those who truly believe. The power of the mind is limitless and is documented not only in the Bible, but in many annals of research. Miracles really do happen. There are so many cases of healings where the physicians had given patients their walking papers to get their house in order. Their cancer was incurable and would send them home to hospice to make them as comfortable as possible. The next visit would indicate a shrinkage or elimination of the tumors altogether. The belief factor is critical but to stay positive is essential. The oncology nurses would tell me they could pick who was going to make it the longest just by their attitude. My sister-in-law, Sheila, had multiple types of cancer at different stages in her life. While going through the chemo treatment she would visualize the game Pacman. She said she would close her eyes and think of the chemo as Pacman going through her body chomping on the cancer cells. She refused to believe differently and is now a ten year cancer free survivor. An oncologist once told her to accept the fact the cancer will return and eventually take her life. She told him to never say that again or I will change oncologists. She was determined to beat the cancer and believed it to be gone for good. She was a big inspiration to me during my recovery period.

I had no idea of the challenges ahead. Thinking positive means believing it as well. There were times when it was very hard to stay focused on the positives since there are so many challenges filling my head. You not only have to worry about beating the cancer, you have to beat the chemotherapy. There are so many variables thrown at you it is hard to stay focused let alone be positive. Each day is a challenge and you really do need to concentrate on it day-to-day. Set your goals for the day and above all keep moving. Don't give in to not eating or resting all day but you do need to listen to your body. Your goals should be simple such as getting out of the house to go to the store once during the day. Go for a drive and enjoy the miracles of life. Remember why you are fighting to stay alive. Above all, remember your support system of family and friends. Some are more supportive and others mean well but just don't say the right things. I always laughed when they said, "your tough you are going to beat this" because there were days when I felt I had little control. I knew I was going to fight by eating right and doing my daily activities on a normal basis.

The first winter was bitter cold as it was one of the coldest winters on record but we still managed to get out of the house. Sometimes we would just go to Costco so I could walk the aisles to get a little exercise. I was on a chemo treatment of leucovorin, 5FU and oxaliplatin. The oxaliplatin would give you a sever reaction to the cold. If I drank anything remotely cool it would burn my throat. If you touched a cold object it was like being stuck to a frozen piece of steel in the winter. Even if I grabbed a refrigerated egg it would be like grabbing an extremely cold metal ball. After three rounds of chemo, I had all I could take of winter, I asked if I could make a trip to Florida just to enjoy the sunny weather. It was just what I needed! The sunshine was therapeutic to my soul and the oxaliplatin. I would still get the reaction but at least when I took a deep breath it was not that cold Ohio air. It was replaced with the Florida heat! One of the nicest things happened to me on my arrival to our condo in Florida. A large group of our friends were waiting for us at the door with balloons and well wishes. It brought tears to my eyes and gave me a special bond from that time forward. I loved my winter family and they knew my struggle. They would be there for me every step with encouragement. We truly were fortunate to have such a great group of friends. I felt miles from the hospital, Ohio and cancer, at least until I got my next scheduled chemo treatment in Florida. I was able to schedule treatment that first year with a center about one mile from the condo. It was very convenient but I came to discover not all treatment centers are the same. You learn as you go or you can take advice from others. The only issue with taking advice from others is everyone has an opinion but none match. This center came highly recommended. That first treatment I learned not all centers are as patient-friendly as the Cleveland Clinic. This center put the patients in a circle in a small room with chairs with the treatment tree next to your chair. This was the extent of the ambiance and charm. The next six hours we all took turn staring at each other as the nurse would come and go with the new bags of chemicals. Patti had to leave and wait for me to call her to pick me up when finished as there was no room for visitors. As soon as I was discharged, I had to go to the cashier where she told me I owed more money. This is when the radar really resonated. Something is wrong with this place but had two more treatments while in Florida. I completed the next treatment with the same routine. I watched as little old ladies were asked to pay additional monies before they were allowed to leave. I wasted no time reporting my findings to my caseworker at Anthem BC/BS. Natalie quickly got involved along with everyone at Florida Blue Cross. It was a low point of my treatment. Thank goodness it was only three treatments and I was assured any additional treatment could be administered at the Cleveland Clinic Weston facility. It was a two hour drive but a small price for peace of mind. It is hard to stay positive when the disease throws you these appalling twists. It is hard enough to fight the cancer but there are so many firms out to make a buck on your misfortunes. You need to do your homework and read the reviews. Dig deep and check the magazines, Better Business Bureaus and journals. We are so fortunate to live close to an institution like the Cleveland Clinic. Not all communities have the choices but always get a second opinion. The security of knowing your team has your best interest in mind can be paramount in your fight to stay positive. You need to believe your group is doing everything to help you fight for the cure.

Always accept help from friends and others if you need it. You are in a fight for your life and will need your energy. Allow friends to help with those little chores so you can reserve some energy to live life. You need to have those little times to remember why you are fighting so hard. There is an overload of negatives being bombarded towards you daily so remember why you want to live. Keep your family and friends close and do those things you really want to do. Rest during the day to attend that dinner party with friends. It is so important to maintain some form of continuity to your daily routine. If you need that rest during the afternoon, take it, but, always try to get out and live a little. I mentioned I would just force myself to go to a grocery store to get out of the house. That actually became very difficult for me as I would run into friends who wanted to stand and chat. I looked healthy so people assume I was feeling good. Nothing could be further from the truth. I looked good from the outside but from the inside looking out I just wanted to go back to bed. There were times it was just too much and I had to go back to the car. Instead of going home, we would go for a ride to ensure I stayed out for a time. The fresh air was good and seeing life all around me made me a little stronger.

It was during my recovery I gained my awareness of the animal life around the house. I relished watching the birds, squirrels and bunnies. I began to focus on getting them to be my friends. I made it a mission to get out of the house to purchase food and seed for my new found friends. There was a new reason to get out of the house, my friends needed and depended on me! Patti was fabulous and she saw through my new found passion. She would suggest to make a run to the store for corn as she was sure the squirrels would like it. Then she would say we should make a run to purchase peanuts for the squirrels. Then she would suggest a run to the feed store to get rabbit food so we can be sure the bunnies are getting fed. It worked, I was getting out of the house with a purpose without just walking up and down the grocer aisles. It took me a while to figure out the reason for Patti's decision to join my new passion. I am not one to be slow on the uptake but we laughed when I finally caught on. She was right, I was getting out of the house to buy supplies and was walking more to put food in the feeders. The point is to find your reason to force yourself to get out of the house. Stay away from the depression settling in your mind and start living again. It is too easy to sit back, feel sorry for yourself and loose some valuable days of life.

We are so fortunate to have friends like Joe and Sue. They constantly called us to get us out of the house. We had a mutual friend, Becky Ballenger, who battled several years with breast cancer before dying from the side effects of the disease. Joe and Sue would arrange for all of us to meet for dinner. Becky was struggling to stay positive as she had so many personal setbacks. Joe would give her the task to find an out of the way restaurant we could enjoy each month. This kept her mind off the cancer and more on living life. It also gave all of us something to look forward to and Becky something to research besides the cancer. It was just another way to get your mind off the disease. You have to continually remind yourself to keep living each day at a time. People are dying all around you but you are still here. Enjoy your time daily as you can never go back and have that time over again. It is not easy facing death while trying to live a full life. I know I cannot plan for a distant future but I certainly can plan for next month's evening with friends. Joe and Sue make sure of that and I love them for it.

12

OUTSIDE NEGATIVES

*E*very cancer is different and every reaction is different. Remember this when even your best intentioned friends say, "stay positive, you are strong and a fighter, did I tell you Steve's sister died of cancer." They really mean well but sometimes their mouths get in the way of their intentions. I learned just because someone else had colon cancer does not mean I will react the same way. Cancer is a very strange disease but staying positive is the biggest cancer fighter of all. I have found it to be as combative as chemo itself. I lost several friends who did not have the family support or the mental attitude to stay positive. My motto continues to be "cancer may take my life, but it will never take a day of living away from me". I wanted to lead my life as normal and as positive as I could. There were some bad days along the way but I still pulled myself off the bed and did something outside the house. We took a lot of rides but stopped at places we used to just drive past. Cancer opened my eyes to a life I was previously just walking through. Cancer opened my eyes to the beauty of Lake Erie and the islands in the distant view. We often would take a ride along the lake as it was a new found solace for me. I was beginning to see the beauty of everything. It was an awakening which is hard to explain. Have you ever driven by a building for years and suddenly noticed its paint color and said wow that looks nice? It has been the same color for years but you just now noticed it. This was happening to me daily. I had a sudden interest in the variety of birds and their beauty.

I found myself enjoying those little gifts from God which I ignored in my pre-cancer life. Feeding the birds, enjoying a good sunset or just absorbing my family going through their own routine day. People go through a continuous cycle of life. While growing up you are constantly looking forward, becoming a teenager, learning to drive, post high school. There was always a next step, a year or two down the road. As an adult you are looking for the career job, searching for that perfect spouse and then too busy trying to make a career to enjoy the daily pleasures of life. Most people look back and say their fondest memories were when they didn't have two nickels but enjoyed the basics of life. They forget they were miserable at the time because they didn't have the money to do the things they would dream about doing. You really never have the time to enjoy your children growing up as most parents get the children in too many activities where it cuts into family time. If you need an activity calendar to stay organized, you may want to step back and reconsider if you have them enrolled in too many events. Of course there are always the exceptions but it is a good time to reflect how your family time is spent. You cannot have this time over. Grandparents love being a grandparent because they have a second chance of family redemption. Not to mention they can just drop the kids off when they become too much.

I was very fortunate to enjoy my family as I was all too aware of the finite time we have in life. My time with my mother was cut short by cancer but my dad made sure he was both mother and father to us. I wanted to ensure my children had those same good family basics. I was taught family comes first, friends will come and go but family is there for life. They are the people who will be there with the most support. It is a blessing if you have friends who offer strong support. I am very lucky to have many great friends who more than manifested themselves during my fight. Don't hesitate to reach out to them for help as most people really do mean it when they say "call me if there is anything we can do". They are just waiting for the call to help. Stay close to those who offer positive support and stay away from those who constantly remind you of your cancer. Surround yourself with those who fill your life with laughter and fun, as laughter really is the best medicine. Cancer can work to your benefit, to change your outlook on your daily activities. Instead of performing a daily routine, look at life from a new perspective. Enjoy your surroundings if you never took the time to notice. Instead of your head being filled with thoughts of cancer, embrace the moments you have and make them as positive as you can.

The negatives will come from the most unexpected origins. It was hard for me to go to the treatment center as I maintained my weight and generally looked good. I would see so many less fortunate that I would walk away a little depressed. The doctors were now becoming less positive with my cure. We exhausted most of the chemotherapy available to me at that time. They virtually told me there was nothing more they could do as my cancer was not responding to treatment anymore. I was always anxious waiting for the call of the blood work results. One of those times I reflected on my past, waiting for what I perceived was an important phone call. I laughed to myself at the comparison. There was nothing like waiting for these calls from the oncologist basically telling you whether you are going to live or die. My CEA numbers kept going up and they finally told me I have approximately one year before the cancer would take over. I could not accept this prognosis and called MD Anderson in Houston for a second opinion and more importantly check for clinical trials available at MD Anderson. This was known as the top facility in the fight against cancer. We scheduled an appointment to establish ourselves for any possible clinical trials. We were told there would be an abundance of local hotels which offer large discounts for MD Anderson patients. The counselor assured us this would not be costly as there were many tools to be utilized. We went through the list but there were no vacancies for the discount program. We decided to just go through the normal reservation process to secure a hotel close to the hospital. We found in order to get the benefits of low price accommodation you have to schedule well in advance. Things were not as they are advertised but we kept going forward. We flew to Houston with great anticipation. That morning we took the cab and entered the front section as instructed by our appointment schedule. I was not prepared for what I was about to see. There were unlimited people in wheel chairs attached to oxygen or chemical drips. They were skeletons of a human being appearing like pictures of the occupants at a concentration camp. It took my breath away and it took everything I had not to cry. I quickly walked the hall to my appointment area. It was a large waiting area filled with hundreds of patients. I sat waiting for my appointment thinking I was not unique. My struggle has been duplicated by thousands of other people. Was this going to be my own destiny, was I fooling myself believing that with positive thinking I was going to be the cancer survivor? So many doubts began to fill my head. The negatives were overwhelming me. How do I stay positive after seeing all of these other patients in the same condition as me?

I began to think all cancers are not the same. Not all people with the same cancer are the same. I didn't know their situation. Maybe I had something they did not have available. I had a great support team. I had a family who loved me. My brother and sister were waiting for my call. I had friends waiting to hear the results of our trip to Houston. I slowly started reviewing my blessings, one by one. It did not come easily and I had to consciously count my blessings. It was a lesson well served. They were very positive as they went through the various testing. At this time the cancer has spread to the lungs, but had too many tumors to perform surgery to have them eradicated at the Cleveland Clinic. The news became even more optimistic when they told us they could perform surgery on a couple of tumors in the lung.

The optimistic news was short lived as they came up with the same conclusion as the Clinic. However, MD Anderson found eleven tumors on the lungs and has also spread to the liver. They told me to get my life in order as the Clinic was wrong regarding a year, they estimated six months at best.

It was a long flight home. How do we tell the family and friends? How do we stay positive going forward? We decided to stick to our motto regarding cancer, "It may take my life but will never take a day away". It was difficult and Patti didn't even want to leave the house that first day. She didn't feel like being happy. I had to remind her people lose their life every day from accidents, heart attacks and other freak ways of death. We were still living and had to live our life on our terms. Bad news was not going to stop us from living the remainder of my life.

Words do matter, especially to a cancer survivor. Each follow up scan can be a life changing event. My experience at MD Anderson made it very hard to stay positive. They filled me with so many doubts of recovery. I could not put my head in the sand any longer. I was not going to survive the cancer. Eventually it was going to take my life. My mindset changed from survival to longevity. If it was going to kill me I was going to fight to stay alive as long as possible. Now I was really taking it a day at a time. I woke up thinking what we can do today to make it a full, fun day. The problem we had is the rest of the world is still living their lives. They are where we were before cancer. Living their lives worrying about the children's schedules, their jobs and all the small stuff which used to consume us. My eyes were opened as these things don't matter. Why doesn't everyone take the time to see the beauty? They are too busy being devoured by the daily chores called life. It is odd but I felt blessed somehow. My eyes have been opened to a new world. It was like a secret world which only I could see. Everything slowed down for me. I was seeing the beauty of my home town which to everyone else's standards is a very plain small Midwestern burg. My first thought was to thank mom, my guardian angel, for giving me this gift. I began to think how much life I wasted up to this moment. I was always in a hurry, held grudges and would say things in anger when it really didn't need to be said at all. My eyes were slowly being opened before my trip to Houston but now it was like I put on a pair of rose colored glasses. I was Pollyanna playing the glad game.

The negatives never stopped coming at me. I still had to shake them off and concentrate on the positives. I was determined to go forward, stronger, without letting them enter my mind. I was beginning to let the negatives get the better of me when I received a call from a good friend. Cherie Oberst lost her husband several years earlier to cancer and had a condo in our association in Florida. We grew up together and knew each other since grade school. She always kept me positive and was like a mother making sure I was sticking to a healthy diet and drinking only lemon flavored water. She went through several years watching her husband suffer without taking proper care of himself. He would take the chemo but then go to a fast food restaurant for lunch. She was determined I was going to do it correctly. She called to tell me of her dream. She asked if I was writing a book or establishing myself on a speaking tour regarding cancer survivors. What an odd question as only a few family members knew I was writing the book on my experiences. She said she saw me standing at a podium giving a speech on staying positive during cancer. There were angels standing behind me smiling nodding their heads in approval. There was one main angel which looked like my mom standing directly behind me with a hand on my shoulder. This gave me the shivers. Cherie knew nothing of my new found knowledge of my mother being my guardian angel or writing the book. I don't see myself as a speaker but I knew it was a sign that I was doing the right thing. I shared my thoughts and she could only scream "Oh my goodness, I really did have a vision." For me, I knew I had to keep writing. There are so many people who need to hear that it is okay to feel down but you have to push to go forward. You can't let cancer take a day away from you.

 I love the water and the pool but my scars were keeping me from one of the things I enjoy. I was letting cancer take that away from me. I was hesitant to take my shirt off in public as I had a scar the length of my torso going in several directions. There were several other smaller scars from the drains and minor surgeries. I finally walked the beach in Florida, as no one I knew would see me. People glanced but no one pointed and laughed either. I didn't know what to expect but was gaining strength to be bold. I decided I would try the pool at our complex. As I should have known, no one said a thing. There was no way they didn't notice, but it was starting to sink in to me that the only person being artificial was me. Why was I concerned about the sight of my scars? I was being too vane and needed to get over myself. I began to easily take off my shirt and had a number of people ask what happened. It did not bother me anymore and I even began to twine a story of a bear attack to amuse myself with people before I would tell the true story. I discovered many of the negatives did not come from the outside but from my own insecurities and thoughts. People are going to do and say things which are mostly innocent in nature. It was up to me not to let it turn into a negative. We once saw an old acquaintance in the waiting room at the hospital and he almost shouted across the room. He was surprised to see me as he thought I was dead. I just smiled and said "I guess you didn't go to my funeral then". It instantly made everyone laugh and turned the negative into a learning moment for everyone.

13

DIET AND OTHER CAUSING AGENTS

Your diet is so important. What goes into your body has such an influence on your body's function. I never realized the truth to the words, "you are what you eat". I ate what I wanted as each commercial on TV made me hungry. After all, I was one of those kids that actually enjoyed the cafeteria food at school. There was very little presented to me that I didn't think was wonderful. Fast food was a joy but the new pre-made foods now made it easier and faster to eat the junk I craved. Everything I liked was bad for me. I knew this but it didn't matter. My, how things change when you finally realize unhealthy food is more than just bad for you. It can change your health in an instant. It can be a slow buildup of poor eating habits for years then quickly manifest itself. People don't realize the effect food has on your total system. Just a month of unhealthy foods can elevate your blood pressure, among other things. Poor eating habits over years will develop many illnesses including cancer. They have linked so many sicknesses to a poor diet over the years, it is a wonder people like me never took the initiative to change their eating habits. The education didn't matter to me, I liked the food and appeared healthy and normal.

Your diet needs to change and there are hundreds of books written by qualified nutritionist, which I am not. It is paramount to find a guide to choose which best fits your interest. I no longer eat the foods I know are unhealthy but for me the damage was done. Years of fast food, convenient foods which probably was not food at all, took its toll on my colon. In addition, I did not exercise on a regular basis. I always scoffed at the joggers as I would say "Show me one that is smiling and I will start jogging." My wife is a walker but I never wanted to go for a walk as there was always something else for me to do. I didn't take the time I needed for me. It was harder to exercise than it is to watch television. I took the easy way out. Exercise is a habit you need to start forming now. It is best to set a daily goal without overdoing it. Establish a new goal each day pushing yourself just a little bit more. Walking or biking are two of the best exercises for people at most any age. The Cleveland Clinic stresses a walking regiment almost immediately after surgery and recommends you continue walking at home. We would go to the mall, grocery store or anywhere if the weather was too bad to walk outside. Early in my recovery we would choose a store where I could use the grocery cart as my walker. I hate to walk so I found the stores were the easiest for me as I had things to take my mind off the walk. In addition, I would run into people which made me stop to talk. This secretly gave me an excuse to stop walking as I would much rather talk to friends than walk. Whatever I was doing was more than if I was sitting watching television.

I was beginning to have a walking routine but also knew my diet needed an overall. I started my research and found there are a few required items to read from the labels on the foods. Prior to cancer I never checked the labels or even knew what to review. I trusted the AMA, the FDA and my government to prohibit manufacturers from making food that may prove to be bad for me. I had no idea there are cancer causing foods. The carcinogens causing cancer proved not only to be in some foods, but in the plates we were eating from. The re-useable plastic containers and bottles were beginning to test positive for some cancers. There are numerous articles where the lab rat died from the testing but the manufacturers assured us there were no issues. We needed to eat or drink more than we were capable to ever get cancer and the results were exaggerated. We even turned a blind eye to smoking because it was proven to make us look cool. The manufacturers spent millions on advertising promoting cigarette use. Everyone wanted to be that guy who picked up the women just by blowing smoke from his cigarettes. We all now know that smoking is a direct cause to cancer. It took a lot of research and court hearings to finally arrive to this truth. Other facts are slowly coming forth on everything around us. It wasn't until I was diagnosed and several surgeries later did I become inquisitive enough to begin doing my own research. It was through this research I came upon a documentary regarding a specific chemical which contains carcinogens directly tied to cancer. This was a government approved chemical used in our carpets, couches, clothes, eating utensils and just about everything we use daily. This cancer causing chemical, which contained PBFE's was introduced as a flame retardant component to children's pajamas after an outbreak of problems. Although the new line of flame resistant clothing made it safer against fire, it introduced a new generation of cancer patients. Although this chemical was found to be very toxic, it was grandfathered for use when other chemicals were banned as cancer causing agents. This chemical found its way into the textile manufacturers for the use in both furniture and carpeting. In our carpets alone there is toluene, benzene, formaldehyde, ethyl benzene, styrene, acetone which cause fetal abnormalities in the test animals. There is also 4-PC used in the backing of carpets. This is one product which is in in almost every home. This is just a one of the many examples of cancer causing agents which is totally approved for use. If you couple this with the furniture manufacturer, dry wall products, kitchen cabinets and clothing, you are attacked daily with the dangerous carcinogens. Not to mention what we are putting in our bodies under the watchful eye of the FDA. I am not a tree hugger by any stretch but I found you really need to be green conscious when looking at carpeting and furniture. The upholstery is very important and can be extremely toxic to your health.

We would discuss at the treatment centers how much cancer there was in the world. It seemed like everyone I spoke to have a family member fighting cancer, fought cancer or lost the battle to cancer. Something had to be the culprit in the dramatic rise of cancer in society. Maybe it was the red car syndrome, but we noticed in almost every village there is a cancer treatment center. The advertisements on TV regarding treatment centers all over the country, all utilizing a different approach to the fight of cancer. You cannot watch television without commercials regarding the treatment of cancer. How did it get so rampant? It was not hard to discover the answer.

Advertising lured us into smoking, drinking, eating fast food without a conscious. We, as a society, enthusiastically ate the convenience food without knowing what it was.

We trusted those in power to be our voice even though we smoked knowing there was a surgeon general's warning on the label. It was not much of a revelation to anyone that the tobacco companies were "hiding" evidence that they knew their product was one of the leading causes of cancer. However, we did not know there was cancer causing agents in almost every aspect of our daily life.

We are just discovering the need to read labels for other items other than calories, carbs or fat content. The first rule of thumb regarding diet is if you don't know what it is don't eat it. If it is a convenience food it is probably not food. It is most probably a genetically made product to simulate the taste of its counterpart. Too many chicken nuggets are probably not chicken at all. Check for GMO or genetically modified organisms. This is food which is genetically enhanced to change the nutritional make-up, taste or smell from its conventional counterpart and should be avoided. Always look for the label which reads Non-GMO. Most food manufacturers, biotechnology companies and the FDA in general do not support the mandatory labeling of GMO when a product was genetically engineered. If it does not specifically say Non-GMO then it probably has been genetically modified. This has been the history of our government watchdog. The lobbyist and large corporations win over the decisions regarding what is allowed to be used in our food source and preservatives.

In the beginning I asked the oncologist if sugar was bad for cancer. He told me that was a misnomer as the sugar is equally transferred to each cell and the cancer cell would not get a larger amount than the noncancerous cells. The part he left out, or didn't know, is that sugar should be avoided entirely by a cancer patient. Most oncologist are not dieticians so do not ask them for their expert advice. If a nutritionist is not available at your treatment center, go directly to your book store or research on your computer. You will find most diet plans indicate sugar is a stimulant to the cancer cell and acidic foods should replace your sugar intake. Items like orange juice, Apple juice, lemons and lemon zesting is good for your PH balance, which is essential in fighting cancer. There are many diets promoting cancer cures including the Gerson Diet, but just knowing what to eat to help promote the cure is helpful. I am not suggesting a diet alone can cure cancer, but there are many studies showing very significant results. I found oncologists have little knowledge regarding the effect of diet on cancer. They are engineered to fight cancer with chemicals not diet.

Your diet is very important in your fight against cancer. You need to do research yourself and you will find there are some vegetables which have been proven to be significant in the remission of cancer. I recommend a very good book on diet and cancer. It is the <u>American Cancer Society Complete Guide to Nutrition for Cancer Survivors</u>. It touches on most foods and preservatives regarding what to eat and which to avoid.

I am a big believer in eating vegetables and fruit and taking supplements in moderation. Cooked broccoli for example is mentioned in almost every diet as essential in reducing cancer. Berries are thought to reduce the risk of cancer. Zesting lemon on your foods are also thought to be an aid in the fight of cancer. This is an area you need to study further as it is such a large part in your battle. I am not a dietician and cannot offer detailed, professional advice. There are many books featuring the benefits of food, herbs and seasoning and how each may affect different cancers. If you decide not to research this yourself, then just eat the basics and avoid the convenient foods. If it comes in a customer convenient container it is probably not your basics. Stick with fish, fresh vegetables and fruit and you will probably hit your goal of eating healthy.

14

THE CONTINUING SAGA CALLED LIFE

"It is not over until it's over."

A great line from Yogi Berra, but never more true than in the fight against cancer. The only problem is, it just seems like it is never over. At least not in your head. The cancer may go into remission or there are no more spots to attack, but every time you get a cold, pain or headache your mind instantly turns to cancer. I am told it takes years of remission before you lose that reaction. Either way, you need to continue your testing and always remain proactive.

Sometimes it is not in your head and the cancer returns. For me, it was never ending as the cancer never took more than a month or two vacation before the CEA markers started increasing leaving us with the task of finding where it landed this time. It took almost three years before my oncologist suggested a molecular make-up to determine which set of protocols we should be using to target my specific cancer. In the past we waited until it landed and then recommended surgery. I was on chemo immediately after my first initial diagnosis and surgery but no follow-up chemo until almost two years later. I am one of those kids that struggled with high school biology. Researching the Internet was very tedious but I found never leave your treatment up to the experts. I would always research and evaluate, but it was not until they told me there was nothing further they could do for me did I begin the pursuit with interest. I used my own intelligence and researched to learn about the treatment of colon cancer. This would work for any specific cancer but if there is anything I have learned is to be your own advocate. The best facilities in the world are not as concerned about your health as much as you are. Once I learned the processes, I was better equipped to make suggestions as to my own treatment. I began asking the questions regarding a molecular make up. It is beneficial to help pick the specific drug to target the cancer. I found the oncologist was taking a wait and see attitude rather than being proactive with the use of chemotherapy. These were a few issues I remedied by being proactive. Although, I was discouraged that the doctors did not do this on their own, I was able to get things going. I really needed to look forward and concentrate on the curing process. You have to be ready mentally to attack the battle that lies ahead and don't dwell on the past. I should have begun my research immediately to hold my caretakers accountable but I knew they do this daily and should have been automatic. Anyone can slip through the cracks so you need to stay on top of your own treatment. We found my particular oncologist tried to always be positive and upbeat. He would rather talk about the weekend than the challenges ahead of me. He was not always discussing the results of the scans leaving me to read them from the charts. It was disheartening to read the CTSCAN report where the radiologist stated the tumors were increasing in size. My oncologist never told me there were any tumors on the report from six months ago let alone suggest they were growing. I was fearful we let too much time go by which could have been spent fighting the growth or spreading of the cells. It was not until he said there was nothing he could do were we able to put a plan of action in place.

Patti discovered there were precautions which a caretaker should be taking when dealing with chemo patients. There was protocol when touching stool or urine when a patient is on chemotherapy. This was never discussed with us. We also read where we should not have sex while on a chemo treatment and had to ask if it was true. This type of education and proactive treatment should be common practice not extraordinary. These are important items for the patient and caregiver and we came across this information by accident several years into our treatment. We also had so many questions about my diet. These were issues we discussed weekly with the oncologist with little feedback. We quickly realized an oncologist was not well versed with nutrition and which foods to eat for a patient with my condition. There are dieticians on staff but you will need to know to ask as they are not always presented for use. It wasn't until I asked about the Gerson Diet did the physician assistant suggest I speak with the dietician when getting my next treatment. She offered a well-balanced diet to fit my colon needs. This would have saved months of soaking in a bath to relieve the pain. We didn't ask if there was a dietician and the information was never presented to us.

These instances are examples to show you must be your own advocate. The best hospitals in the world like the Cleveland Clinic may fail you at times. You need to research the Internet and ask the tough questions. I do not blame the oncologist as there are many forms of treatment and may have already examined them. They see dozens of cases every day and has the formula of protocol for every diagnosis. The questions force them to take the time to thoroughly explain their thought pattern to you, the patient. You don't know what you don't know but need to learn quickly. There is a much needed sense of urgency to learn everything, as much as possible. We learned as we went for two years. We now had to learn what we didn't know. This is when I started having conversations with other patients at the treatment center. We all go through a lot of the same issues and learned so much from them. Simple things like a lemon drop will help to make the food taste normal when on your chemo treatment. Where would you get that information except from another patient?

Through all of this I tried to remain positive. God delivered me through all of those surgeries for a reason. There had to be a purpose to all this pain and medical madness. A little of my spirit would slip away with every negative diagnosis of no hope. It is hard to remain positive when they are offering you a deadline to your life. I only remained optimistic with the help and encouragement of Patti and my family. My brother and sister call me every day to offer support and I feel so blessed to have them in my life. So many families have issues with their siblings but we have none. They offer daily encouragement which has gotten me through some of the dark days. They have no idea how many times doubt was creeping into my spirit when I would get a call from them. My friend, Joe Greco in Canada, calls me daily. It is a quick call but hearing his deep, Godfather like voice is uplifting. Sarah and Nathan usually call multiple times per day. No one knows the importance of a phone call or that get well card. You may never know the spirit of the receiver when they get those words of cheer. A daily call for no particular reason would take me out of negative thought and back into the world of living. My friends, John and Allison Lauer, taught me the value of card giving. Allison is a positive spirit and a cancer survivor herself. She has been fighting for many years yet took the time to send me cards on a monthly basis with a little note of encouragement. Take the time to send a card or make the call as it does make a difference. My personal habits have now changed as I keep a box of get well, sympathy and general cards in my desk. I know how much the simplest of notes meant to me and want to pay it forward from all my friends who took the time out for me.

There were times I would become so lonesome for normalcy I could only break down and cry, but mostly on my own, by myself. I was the one with the smile in public. It does get hard with so much negativity bombarding you. It seemed every movie, every sad story ended with the person dying of cancer. It was all around me, yet it was important to me to stay positive. I would not be truthful if I said I didn't have those thoughts of death. Sometimes I laid in bed in the middle of the night wondering how death was going to manifest itself to me. Will I have much warning? Hopefully there will be little pain. I wonder how it will effect Patti and the kids. I would review each one and determine how much they would miss me. I realized I was at the point there is nothing more we can do. It is just a matter of time. It was going to happen and there was nothing I could do about it. These were not healthy thoughts but I had them. I had to remind myself everyone was going to die. I was going to die anyway, it is just sooner than I would like. I wanted to be there to watch my grandchildren become adults. I was enjoying my children as adults and wanted more time. We had so many plans during retirement which were cut short. All of these negatives entered my mind and I had to work to keep repeating to myself to live my life one day at a time. We needed to enjoy the time we have left whatever the time is. I had to consciously think that I am no different than anyone else. Everyone is in the same category. We are all going to die someday and need to live life one day at a time. We all need to enjoy the daily blessings all around us. Cancer just emphasized that for me. Without cancer I was mentally going through life putting out problems. Sometimes it is a struggle to emphasize the good as I still have to work at being positive and seeing the blessings. I had a few public displays of my emotions with my family, but for the most part I remained the man with a smile.

As I move forward with the cancer, my pain has slowly increased as the discomfort has amplified to affect my daily activity. I don't think anyone really notices, or they don't want to let on they notice. For the most part, I am leading a normal life and excuse my failings to my aging body. I have the normal limitations of a sixty four year old man with a large bucket list. There are some items I know I cannot accomplish. The important thing for me is I don't quit trying.

I recently met a person who was totally cleared of cancer. She went through radiation and chemotherapy for months and finally had a clear scan. She still has her routine follow-up appointments but is cancer free. She instantly went into depression. Her fight was not fought with optimism as she was negative during most of her treatment. There was no talking her out of her negativity. She actually became depressed when she no longer had cancer. I could not figure that out as I am no psychologist. I am sure it has something to do with her being negative during treatment.

If you are going to fight cancer, you may as well carry a positive attitude. I have repeatedly said cancer is not a death sentence. Don't treat it as one. Go forward and enjoy life as no one knows their time. Life was designed that way. There are so many friends and family who have died since my first diagnosis. I had friends diagnosed with cancer after my diagnosis and have already passed away. I have other friends and family members who were seemingly in good health which died instantly. We don't know when we are going to die so live your life daily. I go to funerals and cannot explain why I am still alive and doing well. I read that less than five percent of advanced colon patients live five years. I am one of the blessed ones. I am enjoying what time I have as Cancer may take my life but it won't take a day away from me. Enjoy your days you have and look around at the beauty all around you. It is there if you are brave enough to look. Cancer is a terrible disease but embrace the blessings you received by having the cancer. It is with me daily as I feel the bodily pain it has brought me. There is no relief from its constant reminder yet I relish the squirrels enjoying my corn and the peanuts I feed them daily. My bed table is lined with medications but I never go to sleep without telling Patti how grateful I am to have her by my side. My friends know my pain but the only adjustments we make is the evenings are much shorter. They help me live life daily and I appreciate them for it. I am living my life as if I was cancer free but I now enjoy the blessings I recognize all around me.

My saga continues but I am grateful it does. We plan for the future but not the distant future. Our plans take into consideration what I can physically handle at this point. I have more of a sense of urgency to complete the book as I have more difficult days than good days. The daily struggle continues but always with a smile on my face as I am truly blessed.

My problem list as described by Cleveland Clinic:

Left VATS, LOA pulmonary metastasectomy, rib blocks

Cecal cancer (HCC)

Post-operative pain

Elevate serum creatinine

DVT prophylaxis

DISPOSTION AND FOLLOW UP

Actinic keratosis

Inflamed seborrheic keratosis

Unspecified hypertrophic and atrophic condition of the skin

Aberrant premature complexes

Hypophosphatemia

Postoperative ileus (HCC)

Wound infection after surgery

Sepsis following intra-abdominal surgery (HCC)

Acute postoperative respiratory insufficiency (HCC)

Hypomagnesemia

Acute blood loss anemia

Lactic acidosis

Fecal Peritonitis (HCC)

Intestinal anastomotic leak

Moderate malnutrition (HCC)

Feeding difficulties

Hyperglycemia

Hypercarboa

Bacteremia

Failure to thrive

Hypernatremia

Intraabdominal fluid collection

Colon Cancer (HCC)

Ileostomy

Renal insufficiency

Ventral hernia

Elevated CEA

Colon cancer metastasized to intra-abdominal lymph node (HCC)

Lymphadenopathy, abdominal

Liver metastasis

Secondary malignant neoplasm of liver

Seborrheic keratosis

Sun-damaged skin

Lentigines

Calculus of kidney

ABOUT THE AUTHOR

Jack Rhodes is a five year advanced colon cancer survivor. Less than five percent of identical type cancer patients  survive that long. His determination to fight cancer with a smile has been an inspiration to many people. He is known for his positive attitude although going through seven surgeries within a two year span.

After his first surgery to remove one of the largest tumors recorded at the Cleveland Clinic from his colon he immediately went septic. His chance of survival was less than eight percent. The surgeon called him one of the most stoic people she has ever performed surgery on. Surviving the septicemia the book documents his fears and struggles but also the many blessings he witnesses in his world of cancer. This newfound awareness keeps him optimistic through his ostomy reversal, abdominal reconstruction, and lung and liver surgeries.

The book is filled with extraordinary optimism while displaying the deepest feelings of a person navigating the challenges of cancer. It is a beautiful mix of emotion and humor while educating others directing them through the maze of cancer.

It is a must read for those who are struggling to battle cancer whether newly diagnosed or an experienced survivor.

Made in the USA
Middletown, DE
29 September 2018